Your Guide:
From the Couch
to the Mission Field!

10 steps for Christians over 55 to experience short-term mission trips

Vicky Albaugh

ISBN 978-1-944476-69-4
Also available as an ebook

Scripture taken from the Holy Bible, NEW INTERNATIONAL VERSION®, NIV® Copyright © 1973, 1978, 1984, 2011 by Biblica, Inc.® Used by permission. All rights reserved worldwide.

Cover design by loose-cannon.com
Coffee cup image by Hanny Naibaho on Unsplash

Dedication

I dedicate this book to my loving husband, Dean. You are always by my side in all my projects and adventures. We have had many years together watching the Lord guide us through life. I appreciate your love and support.

Thank you for all you do!

Table of Contents

Introduction

I HAVE BEEN A CHRISTIAN for many years. I accepted the Lord as savior when I was 13. I have always had a dream of traveling the world telling others the good news of Jesus Christ. I have had a few opportunities to travel and proclaim the gospel, but there hasn't been as many as I would like to have. Now that I'm over 55, I feel the urgency to go on more short-term mission trips. I'm writing this handbook as a means to fundraise for my husband's and my mission trips. I would also like to encourage others in my age group to participate in short-term mission trips.

My handbook is written with middle age to elderly Christians in mind. The greatest purpose of this book is to encourage fellow believers to get off the couch, follow their dreams and desires and participate in at least one short-term mission trip in their lifetime. I have listened to many of my friends over the years express their desire to go, but there's always an excuse or a reason why they just can't quite go on a trip. Here's your chance. No more excuses. I will give you many reasons to go and many opportunities for you to grow and learn.

My handbook isn't about theology or to tell you what to think or believe. It is simply one believer to another sharing my faith and opinions about our privilege to tell others about short-term missions and how they can change your life and others around the globe. I have read several books about missions, so some of my viewpoints will reflect information in those books. I have called numerous churches about short-term missions and I will also include information from them. I will include a list of books in the spiritual prep chapter so you can also read and learn from those books.

For this handbook, the definition of a short-term mission trip will be a one or two-week trip with the purpose to spread the gospel at home and abroad. This handbook will be helpful to anyone; however, I will be referring to Christians 55 and older. There seems to be a lot of information for young people going on trips, but not so much for the 55 plus group that still desire to serve in this capacity on the mission field.

Section 1

Researching and deciding about going on a trip

Chapter 1
How do we decide who should go or if we should go?

ACTUALLY, ANYONE WITH A TESTIMONY of Jesus Christ as savior and an open heart can go. It's really as simple as that, but we will explore many things to think about before making a decision. Let's look at two of the best missionary scriptures in the Bible.

Mark 16:15 Jesus said, "Go into all the world and preach the gospel to every creature."

Matthew 28:16-20 "Then the 11 disciples went to Galilee, to the mountain where Jesus had told them to go. When they saw him, they worshipped him; but some doubted. Then Jesus came to them and said, "All authority in heaven and on earth has been given to me. Therefore, go and make disciples of all nations, baptizing them in the name of the Father and of the Son and of the Holy Spirit, and teaching them to obey everything I have commanded you. And surely, I am with you always, to the very end of the age."

What is the true purpose of the church? What is the true purpose of being a believer? God is calling all of us imperfect people, to bring about His glory. Please first take the time to pray and ask for guidance. Some of you may say you can't physically go on a trip. That's fine, you can pray for missionaries and support those that are called to full time missions and others participating in short-term mission trips. Let's evaluate what has happened to the church in America. Many of us have grown up in church and have seen things change over the years. I have noticed that some churches believe they need to provide entertainment and performances and have programs in order to draw in new people to the church. Whatever happened to preaching the Word of God and making disciples as Christ commanded in Matthew 28:19?

So, you may be thinking that no one is going on short-term mission trips. That's definitely not true. According to the book, *Helping without Hurting in STM*, they say there are two to three million Americans each year going on international trips. The average cost of a trip is $1500. We are going on trips, actually millions of us are going. What are some of the personal reasons people choose to go?

1. They have concern for the Great Commission and lost souls.

2. They are being obedient to God's word.

3. They have compassion for those who have never heard the gospel.

4. Practical reasons include: adventure or escaping problems at home.

After people return from a trip, you hear how the trip changed their lives. Here are a few things that you may learn and help you grow in your relationship with Christ.

1. You may learn about yourself and what is important.

2. You may learn what things you can live with or without.

3. You may learn about others and their needs and culture.

4. You may learn about your own culture and the pros and cons of it.

5. You may learn about your strengths, weaknesses, character, your gifts, talents and shortcomings.

Don't try to over analyze you and your life and say God can't use you. Remember, God uses imperfect people as we see in the Bible. Here are 2 examples:

1. Jeremiah
Jeremiah 1:6-7 Ah, Sovereign Lord, "I said, I do not know how to speak; I am only a child." But the Lord said to me, "Do not say, 'I am only a child.' You must go to everyone I send you to and say whatever I command you."

2. Timothy
I Timothy 4:12   "Don't let anyone look down on you because you are young, but set an example for the believers in speech, in life, in love, in faith and purity".

I Corinthians 1:27-29
God chose the foolish things of the world to shame the wise; God chose the weak things of the world to shame the strong. He chose the lowly things of this world and the despised things - and the things that are not - to nullify the things that are, so that no one can boast before him.

These are examples that show us that because of Christ, we are all able to be used to make disciples. Please pray and seek guidance from the Lord. There are many scriptures that promise He will give us wisdom when we're seeking and asking for it. My favorite scripture is Proverbs 3:5-7.

As we know or presume, there are thousands of people daily who die who did not trust Jesus Christ as their Savior. According to the book, *How to Plan and Prepare for Short Term Missions*, it has been estimated that 168,000 people die every day without knowing Christ as savior. In the same book it tells us that multitudes of people have never heard the Good News of Jesus Christ, yet the command to preach the gospel to every creature has never been cancelled. So, we can all ask ourselves what we are doing about the command. Do we continue to live just for ourselves or do we do something about it?

I am writing this handbook specifically for Christians 55 years and older because my husband and I are over 55 and would really like to be more involved in short-term missions. I believe people our age have much to offer. We are more mature and are free from many responsibilities that younger persons have in their lives. For many of us, our children are grown and some of us are retired or have been able to cut back our full-time careers. According to the Entrepreneur Magazine, people over 50 make excellent employees as well as excellent participants on short-term missions. Here are the 12 benefits that were listed in their article called, "*12 Benefits of hiring Older Workers*".

1. Dedicated. They produce higher quality work. They're able to find potentially costly mistakes made by younger workers.

2. Punctual. Most older workers look forward to work and are punctual.

3. Honest. As a group they possess values or personal integrity and a devotion to truth.

4. Detail-oriented, focused and attentive. These details can rub off on the younger workers. Many businesses have saved money due to these traits.

5. Good listeners. Most of the time they have learned to listen and only need to be told once how to do a task.

6. Pride in a job well done. Older workers are more willingly to stay later to get a job done because of their sense of pride in their final product.

7. Organizational skills. Older workers are more organized just because of their experience. Stats on workplaces say that more than one million-man hours are lost each year simply due to workplace disorganization.

8. Efficiency and confidence. Older workers have confidence in sharing their ideas with management and this in turn helps companies to be more efficient.

9. Maturity. Years of experience handling people's problems help them keep calm when things get stressful.

10. Setting an example. Older workers make excellent mentors and role models which makes training new employees less difficult.

11. Communication skills. Through years of experience they have learned how to convey their ideas to the boss more effectively.

12. Reduced labor cost. Many older workers already have their retirement savings or they just desire to work in a field where they have passion. Consequently, many of them will work for less money and accomplish more on a job that is their passion.

As you can see, there are many reasons for you and I to get off the couch and go to the mission field. I will continue to explain what short-term missions are and how they are organized. Please keep reading, keep praying and see where the Lord leads you in Short Term Missions!

Chapter 2
What is a short-term mission trip?

A SHORT-TERM MISSION trip is a group of Christians traveling to another location for the purpose of proclaiming the gospel of Jesus Christ. Many trips will participate in humanitarian aid also. For the purpose of this handbook, I will be referring to trips that are 1-2 weeks in length. Short-term missions can be for 1 to 2 years and for any age. They can also be close to home or in any foreign country. The participants can choose to go on a trip with a mission organization, with a local church or on their own. The purpose usually includes at least one of the following and many include 2 or more.

1. Preach the gospel. This can include any or all of the following: Evangelism, church planting and teaching to the body of Christ.

2. Humanitarian aid. This can include the following: Feeding the poor, Building churches and houses, looking after orphans and widows, visiting those in prison and providing education.

Jesus does command us to provide humanitarian aid as we read in Matthew 25:35-46

"I tell you the truth, whatever you did for one of the least of these brothers of mine, you did for me"

3. Developmental aid. This kind of aid assists communities

in areas of development and usually includes: building programs, education, agriculture techniques, building water wells etc. These should be long term solutions to underlying socio-economic factors. These programs give short-term mission members a chance to develop long-term relationships with the communities they help.

Humanitarian and developmental aid is important. Jesus did command us to help the least of these. We must be careful to give them a hand up and not a hand out. Hand-outs are important in times of crisis which can include disastrous storms, famine or war. At any other time, it's a good idea to come alongside the community and provide a hand up. For example, a hand up can be farm animals, agriculture tools and education, seeds and techniques for planting. Anything that can help the community become self-sustaining. Another idea includes helping them start a community bank in order for them to make micro loans to people starting a business. We need to keep in mind whether we are helping or hurting the communities. In many cultures around the world, the men are expected to take care of their families. However, in regions that have been hit by war, famine, disease and storms, there are many orphans and widows. Again, we are commanded to help these as seen in James: 1:27. "Religion that God our Father accepts as pure and faultless is this: to look after orphans and widows in their distress and to keep oneself from being polluted by the world. "

4. Fellowship, learning and encouragement. I really enjoyed reading and I learned a lot from the book, *Helping without Hurting In Short Term Missions.* This book really approached missions from a different viewpoint. It talks about how all of us are broken and we all contribute to poverty in this world. Basically, poverty is complicated. I would invite you to read the book. How can we help the world and its poverty? We can't fix their circumstances. But we can go and encourage them in their Christian faith,

affirm the greatness of God, show dignity for the poor and relate to them with all of our mutual need for Christ. Just because we don't live in poverty doesn't mean that we're not also broken without Christ. We also need to leave our god complexes at home. It helps if we are committed to learning about their history and culture. Poverty is complicated, so remember alleviation is a long-term goal. Let the local Christians guide you with projects. Allow them to solve their problems. Let's truly be a blessing. We don't always have to be in control or tell them how they need help. Pray and ask for guidance. Churches in foreign countries feel blessed and grateful to just have you there with them. Let's go and be a blessing to others. Form long-term relationships and you will see how the Lord uses them and us for good, for His glory.

Chapter 3
How do I know if I'm ready to go on a trip?

THE THREE PRIMARY SOURCES of mission trips are either national missionary organizations or local churches. A few people venture out on their own but that's not recommended. Whichever way you choose, your first goal will be to go as a helper to serve others and the Lord. There are quite a few national organizations. You can do an internet search for short term mission trips and you will find quite a few.

There is a great website with many resources called www.shorttermmissions.com. They have approximately 1,700 trips listed with 113 organizations. Most organizations in their trip fee includes housing, food and transportation to and from the airport. There will usually be extra charges for health insurance while on the trip and your airfare. If you pay your fee and those additional expenses, everything else for the trip is covered. You will see options for airfare later in the handbook.

When choosing an organization, remember that you're not going on a vacation. We all have different roles to play on a short-term mission. They try to match your skills to their needs on their trips. Each organization will offer many trips to many countries. You can find most of this information on their website. The website will tell you what kind of work they'll be doing and you should be able to decide if you have those skills.

Another point to consider with an organization is their vision and belief system. I'm keeping this handbook non-denominational, but there are differences in our Christian doctrine. Read their statements of faith in order to see if you can work alongside them. Here are a few suggestions for you when choosing a missions organization.

1. Pray for wisdom and guidance in choosing the right organization.

2. Study their website and FAQ's in order to see their vision and belief system.

3. Call or email with any and all of your questions.

4. Find out the total cost of the trip. Does it include trip cancellation insurance or out of country health insurance or evacuation insurance?

5. Do they allow any days off for sightseeing?

Pray and feel confident about the organization you choose. Continue to pray for God's guidance and perfect will for your trip.

Another option for choosing a trip is with your church or a friend's church. Many churches have ongoing relationships with foreign churches or ministries. A positive point for going with your church is that you already know people and if you don't, you can continue a new friendship after the trip. You already know you are like minded in your beliefs. Also, many churches go back to the same countries, same churches overseas and they already have relationships. That makes it easier for you on your first short-term mission trip.

One of the cons of going with a church is the leadership. Many times the people that participate on a trip changes from year to year. So, this is where we all need to be flexible. The duties of the leader may vary. The leader may be responsible for food, lodging and work project. Or the church may share these responsibilities with the pastor and members of the host church or ministry.

How can you assess if you are ready? What does it take to go on a missions trip? We all are called to go or contribute to missions. However, you can ask yourself a few questions. You do want to make sure your trip is worthwhile to you and those you are serving. Ask yourself the following questions to assess your spiritual readiness:

1. Am I a Christian?

2. Am I faithful with my Bible devotions and church attendance?

3. Do I desire to share the Good News with others?

Here are two questions for your physical readiness:

1. Do I have health problems or a medical condition that may get worse on a trip or may endanger my life?

2. Am I unhealthy and have addictions to cigarettes or alcohol? If yes, do I need to get help with these issues before going on a trip?

Here are two more general questions to assess your readiness to participate:

1. Do I know why I want to go?

2. Do I realize it's not a vacation and I'll be working with people relatively unknown to me and there will be stresses?

I can't tell you the right answers for you. Please answer them truthfully and pray and decide if you're ready to go on a short-term mission trip.

Here is a list of a few more things you will want to consider when traveling internationally.

1. Is your passport current? Best practice is to have it valid for at least 6 months after your return. Do you need a Visa?

2. Is there political unrest? Will it be safe for a team to travel there?

3. What diseases are prevalent? How likely is it to get

Malaria? Are there outbreaks of SARS, bird flu, swine flu, Ebola or Zika Virus? What about the preventable diseases? Are they having an outbreak of cholera, TB, Yellow fever, chicken pox, measles or mumps?

Not all these diseases will be prevalent in all countries at all times. Check with your mission organization or the leader of the church trip to see if they know what shots and meds you need. If they don't know, you can ask your Primary Care Doctor. You can also look it up on the CDC website for the country you are traveling. I have included information in this handbook about looking up this information on the CDC website.

4. Are there US government warnings for a travel ban for your country?

As you can see, it is very exciting to be thinking about being a participant on a short-term mission trip. Just think, you could be half way around the world making a difference and showing the love of Christ to the church and the lost. I know there are many things to think about when choosing a short-term mission trip. You can go with a national mission organization or with a local church. Then think about a few questions about your readiness to go and be aware of traveling hazards, then you can decide. Don't get overwhelmed or afraid. Have faith and God will use you and bless you. Most people come back feeling they received more than what they gave to the host country/church/ministry. It definitely works both ways. Please be open and ask the Lord to lead you!

Chapter 4
Should we go? Is it worth the cost?

I'VE ALWAYS HAD A DESIRE to be a missionary. I started going on short-term mission trips with my kids and their youth groups starting in 2001.   I went for five years with my sons to the Navajo Nation in AZ and NM as part of a youth missions program with the Nazarene church. Now that I'm older, I started thinking about going again on short term missions. My husband and I were able to go a couple of years ago to Honduras with a church in the Sacramento area. We helped with construction on a Christian school and we held a medical clinic to help the community. Those experiences were great. I felt that I had made a difference in those people's lives for Christ.   My dream is to help others and proclaim Christ throughout the world. Then I started to wonder if it is worth all the time and all the money that it takes to go on these trips. I started reading missions books. Through these books and the Holy Spirit, I have come to the conclusion that it is worth every minute and every dollar that we invest.

I've mentioned before in this handbook reasons to go on a trip. Now we'll explore some of the cons as well as other pros. You will be able to decide for yourselves if it's worth the cost. If you look at numbers and stats about mission trips, you may question the need. Again, from the book, *Helping without Hurting in Short Term Missions*, here are the numbers and the statistics:

1. Between two and three million people from the US go on a short-term missions each year. (as of 2010)

2. 20 - 25% of all church members will likely go on an international short-term mission trip in their life time. (as of 2009)

3. $1,370 - $1.450 per person is an average cost.

Does that mean that we don't need to go on trips? Does that mean that we should just send money to the full-time missionaries and pray for them? In my opinion, I think we should still go. It's not about what we can do in 1-2 weeks but what we can learn and the knowledge we gain that leads to spiritual growth. We are all broken due to sin. Instead of us wanting to fix poverty around the world, maybe we could all enjoy fellowship together and affirm our mutual need for Christ in all of our lives.

Having said all that, there are still ways that we can be more harmful than good when we go on these trips. I will list a few and you may be able to add a few more.

1. Little to no time in preparation for the trip.

2. No understanding of the culture or their lack of resources.

3. No preparing with vaccinations or medicines needed for the country.

4. Arrogance and selfishness during the trip.

5. No support for the local church. Not willing to listen and cooperate.

6. No foresight into whether or not they can maintain equipment you brought for them.

7. Inflexibility. Not able to change to a different project when necessary.

You may go to Africa or anywhere in the world and have certain plans to build a church or do a Vacation Bible School. However, it may not go as planned. Their goals may not be your goals. When you are visiting another country, their culture may be disorienting and overwhelming to you. Be prepared to not accomplish your goals. You may also be waiting for some great spiritual experience to happen also. Just go with the flow and don't force spiritual incidents either. Take a long-term view on your trip and experience. See how you are just one piece of a puzzle. We all feel like we get so much out of these trips, but you may go and feel like nothing changed for you. That's ok because things will continue to happen when you go home. Allow the Lord to use the experience for long term growth in your life. Let's be obedient and go with the goals of listening, learning and fellowship with believers. Trust the Lord and He will work in your life and their lives.

Ultimately we have a responsibility to "Do Unto Others Well" as Jesus tells us in Matthew 7:12 "So in everything, do to others what you would have them do to you, for this sums up the Law and the Prophets." The Holy Spirit is the author of change in our hearts and in the hearts of His people wherever we are called to serve. However, we do have a responsibility to make this investment count for His Kingdom. Each trip cost approximately $1,500 and months of preparation for us and about four weeks of prep and cleanup for the host ministry. So, we do want to look at ways this trip can and should influence our lives and produce long term consequences.

1. The experience reminds us to pray for missions around the world.

2. The experience helps us to become advocates for lost souls.

3. The experience opens our eyes to see the need for financial support for local ministries and abroad.

4. The experience helps us to be a loving voice to all.

5. The experience helps us explore God's work in the world. It helps us be more aware of the needs and helps us

to be more compassionate.

6. The experience continues to help us grow in faith and see God transform our lives.

Remember we aren't alone in our desire to see others know Christ as Savior. On these trips we have the privilege to walk beside our brothers and sisters to bring about the glory of Christ. We all come from different places and different cultures, but we are united in Christ. God has given this trip to us as a blessing and investment. So, whatever the circumstances while we are with the host, let's be a blessing to them.

The remainder of this handbook is how to plan and go on a trip. You'll be learning different ways to fundraise, what to pack, how to find an airline and how to prepare spiritually. Then I'll give you a few tips for while you are on the ground with the host and then we'll get you home from a really great trip that hopefully, you will remember for the rest of your life.

Section 2

Preparing for your trip

Time frame is 6 months to 1 year plus before your trip

Chapter 5
Time to choose a trip

THIS HANDBOOK IS FOR THE CHRISTIAN over 55 years who may or may not have ever gone on a short-term mission trip. I will give you an overview of the whole process of planning and going on a trip. Some things may not apply to every trip. Many churches and organizations will do these steps for you. You never know when you may want to lead a team or the leader may need assistance.

So that I wasn't relying solely on my experience, I decided to interview church short-term mission leaders and missionaries in order to see what groups are doing and what missionaries are desiring from the groups that come to help. My friend, Marissa Young and myself spoke to approximately 20 leaders and missionaries and had them answer questions on a survey for me. I will be referring to my surveys in this part of the book. It isn't a scientific survey, but the participants were from all over the US and the missionaries were from various countries. At the end of this handbook, I will summarize their answers. I really appreciate all of them participating. I want to thank Marissa also for making phone calls and sending emails in order to get these surveys done.

Since this is a handbook for all of us over the age of 55, let's look at some practical things to consider when choosing a mission trip. Remember, there are trips all over the world, near and far. Let's try to be practical when we are choosing so we can be successful and make an impact. Make sure you can physically do whatever your projects will be on your trip. If you're not sure you are physically strong enough to participate, start preparing at least six months ahead of the trip. Since it is unpredictable everything that will happen on your trip, prepare for long days standing or walking. Try to exercise at least 30 minutes per day to increase your endurance.

It's time to pick a trip!

Keep everything in mind when choosing. Here are some questions to ask yourself before deciding.

1. What kind of projects am I prepared for?

2. Am I physically able to take the trip and do the work?

3. Do I want to go with a group from a missions organization or with a local church group?

4. You can find over 1000 mission trips listed at www.shorttermmissions.com

5. How long of trip should I choose? When we refer to a short-term mission trip, we'll be referring to 1-2 weeks.

6. Have I been praying and asking the Lord for His will concerning which trip I should take?

OK, you've decided on your trip! Congratulations!

Here are the 10 steps that it takes to go on a Short-term Mission trip and approximate timetable:

Do the following 6 months – 1 year plus ahead of trip

1. CHOOSE your trip.

2. RESEARCH overseas travel requirements. This includes passports, visas, immunizations and meds.

3. TRAVEL ARRANGEMENTS: Airfare and lodging. Travel Health Insurance and Trip cancellation insurance.

4. RAISE support and start fundraising.

Do the following 2-6 months ahead of trip

5. PREPARE spiritually and culturally. Pray for your trip. Learn about country's culture and history. Attend group prep meetings.

6. Make your PACKING and shopping lists.

Do the following the last month ahead of trip

7. Explore your CELL PHONE OPTIONS for using your cell phone overseas.

8. GET IT Done!

- Get your shots and meds
- Get your travel insurance
- Get your cell phone plan
- Get your gadgets and clothing

9. GET PACKED!

10. LAST MINUTE TO DO LIST. 10 things to do to prepare for your trip and for leaving home.

GO ON YOUR TRIP! BE A BLESSING TO OTHERS!

Chapter 6
Research overseas travel requirements

INCLUDING PASSPORTS, Visas, Vaccines and medicines

1. Check to see if your passport will be valid for 6 six months after your trip.

2. Check to see if your host country requires a visa.

3. Check to see what vaccines and medicines are recommended.

Let's start with the basics. What is a passport? It's a travel document that serves as the ultimate form of proof for your citizenship. US passports are issued by the US Department of State. What is a travel visa? An official government document that temporarily authorizes you into the country you are visiting. A visa is issued by the government of your host country. It is usually issued in the form of a stamp in your passport, but it may be a paper document or an electronic document. Visas may be revoked at any time. Many countries require exit visas also.

As of January 2017, US passport holders could travel to 174 countries and territories visa free or obtain a visa upon arrival. US is ranked third in terms of travel freedom according to *Hinley Visa Restrictions Index*. To see what the visa requirements for your visiting country, go to www.passportsandvisas.com. On the home page click on "travel visas". Then from the dropdown box, choose "I'm traveling to:" and pick your country. Then on your country page it has a chart that will tell you what kind of visas are issued such as business, tourist or student. It will tell you if a visa is required, some basic information about the visa and then the approximate date you will receive it. So, whether you need a passport or visa, start early.

What vaccines and medicines are required for your visiting country?

Go to CDC.gov website. On the home page, click on the menu. The menu drops down and you click on "travelers health". The left side of the screen is for travelers. It will ask you "where are you going?" Select your country from the list. Under the dropdown box, it does ask, What kind of traveler are you? There are boxes for tourist and mission/disaster relief. You can check either one. Long term missionaries need to pick the mission one. After that, click on the green bar that says, GO.

There are five main categories under each country. The first one is "Vaccines and Medicines". Under that, you will find out what vaccines and medicines you need for your trip and why. The second box is "Stay healthy and safe". This section helps you with food and water safety and bug bites. You may Click on each sub category under each box for more information about your country. The third box is "Healthy travel packing list". Some of these items may not apply to your personal health, so disregard. The fourth box is "Travel Health notices". A big notice right now is about the Zika virus and the countries affected by it. The fifth box is "After the trip". If you click on the link for "Getting sick after travel", you will get information about what to do for certain conditions when you return home. Some of the things the list includes: fever, persistent diarrhea and skin problems.

I looked up information on El Salvador. The CDC always recommend the routine vaccines. The routine vaccines are: MMR, DTP, chicken pox, polio and the yearly flu shot. They may want you to get a Hep A or Hep B series. A Hep B vaccine series is usually given as a series of three or four shots over six months period. This is why I'm having you research what vaccines are needed at least six months before your trip. When you do your research and you know you haven't had any Hep B shots, call your doctor or travel clinic and get started on that. The other vaccines won't be needed as soon. Your doctor may or may not be able to give you the travel vaccines and medicines. If you call your doctor and they say they don't do any travel medicine, you can look for a travel clinic in your area.

A travel clinic is a medical facility that specializes in providing preventive medical care for travelers. They don't only give you the vaccines, medicine for malaria and diarrhea, but they give you advice on how to prevent infections, how to avoid insect bites and how to consume safe food and water. So, they are a very good travel resource for you.

I did a Google search for "travel clinic" in my area, which is Sacramento. One of my results was Passport Health USA. You can find them on the internet at: http://passporthealthusa.com Go to their website and you can put your zip code in to get the closest clinic to you.

Not every travel clinic provides the yellow fever vaccine. You need to go to an authorized center. You can find a center by looking on the internet at vaccines.gov/travel. Look under the second section, "Where to find travel vaccines", and under the last bullet point, click on "authorized center". You can check with your travel clinic first to see if they can get this for you.

Takeaways:

- Make sure your passport will be valid for six months and travel visa will be valid for three months after travel

- Make sure you start applying for your passport renewal, passport or travel visa at least three months before traveling

- Make sure you start your vaccinations six months ahead if you need any of the Hep B series.

Chapter 7
Travel and lodging arrangements

FROM THE ANSWERS TO my surveys concerning air travel, there was a broad range of solutions. Some groups researched the internet for the best deals while others used a travel agency. Also, some of the mission organizations did the planning for the group. Some groups did make their own arrangements. The locals can suggest van companies and lodging. They may also help you navigate public transportation if this is your best way to get around while in their country.

Tips for planning your own airfare and lodging:

Airlines

1. Do you have a travel credit card and you've been earning points towards a trip? Try to use your points towards this trip.

2. You can also use a reputable travel agent to book for you. Travel agents can book groups and you will be able to make payments instead of paying everything upfront. If you don't know a travel agent, I can help you. Email me at travel55plus@gmail.com.

3. Compare prices on comparative websites. Set up e-mail alerts so you can see if prices are going up or down.

4. Do you want a budget airline or premium? Sometimes it's worth paying a little extra to get better service.

5. Try to book your flight in sections. Sometimes it's cheaper. You can go part way and then have a break. It helps to break up the flights when flying anywhere in Asia.

If you don't break up the flights, try using transit hotels.

A transit hotel is a short stay hotel typically used at international airports. People can check into them if they have at least six hours between flights for a nap and a shower. The transit hotels are mostly in Asia and the most popular one is in Singapore.

A few of the airports having transit hotels are: Singapore, Malaysia, S. Korea, Thailand, UAE, The Netherlands, Prague Czech, Switzerland and New Delhi, India.

Do an internet search for your desired location. I searched for "airport hotel" in Madrid, Spain. The following is the description of their airport hotel:

Air rooms – There are 22 rooms located inside terminal 4 on floor one(land side). Rooms can be booked for day use (3-6 hours) between 10 a.m. and 6 p.m. or overnight. Showers are available. A shower kit consisting of a towel, gel and slippers are provided.

Travel agency is another choice for the group or individual to plan their airfare. Travel agents do have access to fares and deals that are not available to the public. They can quote airfare for individuals or for groups of 10 or more. If you buy individually, each person has to pay when they book the flight. If you book as a group, each person puts down a deposit and the balance is usually due 45 days before your trip.

Lodging

From all the people I have spoken to concerning their short-term mission trips, I would say about 90% of them stay at the local church or with people from the ministry.

Just in case you need to plan your own lodging, here are some tips.

1. Make sure you pick a location close to the ministry or church.

2. Read reviews online and make sure you will feel safe.

3. Make sure transportation is available for you to and from your working locations.

4. Work with a travel agent to find transportation and safe lodging. If you don't know an agent, please email Vicky at travel55plus@gmail.com.

Trip Health insurance and trip cancellation insurance

I've been reading a lot about travel health insurance and trip cancellation or cancel for any reason. There are major differences. The travel health insurance is what you buy for $30 for 30 days or less. This coverage is with Trip Armor. If you purchase trip cancellation or cancel for any reason, that will cost you more. The cost will be determined by your trip cost and your age.

Here are several things an insurance policy should do when you buy one for your short-term mission trip.

1. Medical Insurance – More than likely your health insurance plan won't cover you overseas.

2. Emergency evacuation coverage. This can be used if you need to be evacuated home or to another city or country for sickness or injury. Some countries will not be able to provide you with adequate medical care and you'll need to be evacuated.

3. Repatriation of remains. Your visiting country will return your body in case you died while on your trip.

4. Trip Interruption. If you have changes to your trip once you are traveling, the insurance will pay for the changes to either get you to your destination or home.

I did chat with a rep from missiontripinsurance.com. I was asking how would I access medical care in other countries and if I would need to pay for it until the insurance company reimbursed me. She did tell me to keep receipts for all the little expenses and seek medical help first before stressing about using the insurance. You will want to have the customer care number with you to call about any services. The insurance company will work directly with the hospital and any larger expenses. Trip Armor is the plan that I was using to ask questions. It covers all of the above benefits. I'm planning to get this for all of my trips. At the time of my writing this book, Trip Armor cost $30 for a trip of 30 days or less. You never know what will happen while you are gone and it is worth the peace of mind.

After speaking to the insurance rep about Trip Armor, I began wondering what trip cancellation and cancel for any reason covers. This coverage is in addition to your $30 health insurance policy for Trip Armor. The trip cancellation is insurance against something coming up before your trip that will prevent you from traveling. You need to apply for this coverage and they will give you a quote based on your trip cost and your age. You must also put in a claim at least 2 days before your departure date. Reimbursement on your trip is usually around 70%. So, if you want that kind of coverage, that will be in addition to the $30 Trip Armor policy.

Travel insurance should be a very high priority when going on a short-term mission trip. I read one book that said don't even go on the trip if you can't afford the insurance. Of course, this is your decision unless your group requires you to purchase it. If you end up sick or injured without insurance, you could be financially devastated. Travel insurance will help pay for accidents, emergency medical care and even evacuate you to another country if your visiting country can't provide care for you. It will even cover non-medical emergencies. It covers evacuation in case there is political unrest, it covers travel delays, lost or delayed baggage. Trip Armor covers all of the above and more. Get on missiontripinsurance.com for all the details.

I do want to mention a story about my friend and her son that was traveling to Florida to get on a cruise. She did purchase the trip insurance for her cruise. Her son was severely sick when their plane landed in Phoenix on their way to Florida.

It took all day and evening for them to get a flight back to Sacramento. She wasn't worried about the cost of the cruise at this point, but it was expensive. After her son received medical care and began to start feeling better, she filed a claim to get a refund on her cruise.

I am happy to report that the trip insurance worked and she received a full refund from the cruise company! So, it was definitely a wise decision to get the trip cancellation policy.

Takeaways:

- Good idea to get travel insurance in case you get sick or an emergency happens while gone in a foreign country.

Chapter 8
Raising support and fundraising

THERE ARE MANY WAYS of financing your trip. The Lord will provide. Here are a few scriptures that remind us of that.

Romans 13:8
Let no debt remain outstanding, except the continuing debt to love one another, for he who loves his fellow man has fulfilled the law.

Philippians 4:19
And my God will meet all your needs according to his glorious riches in Christ Jesus.

2 Corinthians 9:8
And God is able to make all grace abound to you, so that in all things at all times, having all that you need, you will abound in every good work.

Always pray and see how the Lord will provide and bless you! Here are 3 possible ways:

1. You can use your savings or work extra shifts or jobs. Some people prefer to make sacrifices to either save more money or to work extra. The Bible does talk about Paul

being a tent maker to pay his own way. (Acts 18:1-3, and 2 Thes. 3:7-9). Some people that are 55 and older are living on retirement benefits and feel this is a good way to use some of their savings. I wrote this book to fundraise for my husband and I to go on trips.

2. Ask churches and friends to provide support for you. Send out support letters to family and friends explaining your reasons for participating in your short-term mission trip. Not everyone is comfortable with asking, but it does allow others to support you and receive that blessing of sending you to share the good news of Jesus Christ.

3. Last but not least is doing fundraisers. You can either do them individually or as a group. Some ideas are bake sales, car washes and sponsored walks. My friend, Melissa Chapel is great at fundraising for church events and ministries. I'm including her top 5 fundraising ideas:

> 1. **Craft/Vendor Fair**. You sell booth spaces to crafters, home based businesses and local small businesses. Booth fees can range anywhere from $25 to $200 per day depending on the size, quality of advertising and the venue.
>
> Choose a theme and have some fun. These can be simple and nice and still amount to a good amount of money for the amount of work. Be sure to have a booth about your mission trip or project. If you don't have a church building, think outside the box and check into having your fair at a local park, town hall etc.
>
> 2. **Yard/Rummage Sale**. Yes, I hear the groans but there is a reason they have been around forever…..people LOVE them and they make money!! With a little organizing along the way it can be smooth sailing and a lot of fun. Here are hints that Melissa learned along the way and make you more than a few bucks.

a. Sort your items ahead of time. Have a big get together a couple of days ahead. Clean, group and sort the items. People like junk but don't want dirt or grime.

b. Have a potluck at the same time as the cleaning, this encourages people to show up and helps build and strengthen relationships.

c. If you have a bunch of small items, put them into small plastic bags and sell them by the bag. It will give you and the customer more value.

d. If you have tons of clothes, sell them by the bag.

e. When getting close to the end of the sale, be creative and have a clearance sale.

3. **Sell Thirty-one gifts**. Melissa is a consultant for them. You can find her website at www.mythirtyone.com /MilliChapel. Thirty-one gifts is one of the top direct sales companies in the nation. They are a wonderful company that empowers women to stand on Christian values. It has incorporated these values into their business model enabling women to live out their lives as Proverbs 31 women. They offer groups many fundraising programs. I encourage you to check them out!

4. **Drive-thru Dinners**. Drive-thru dinners are a presale Family Meal that is hot and ready for pick up. You select a menu. For example, here is one I've done: BBQ Tri tip, green salad with Italian dressing, baked beans and French bread. I presold tickets for $25 for a family of 4. I did prepare a few extra meals, but it is highly recommended to have people preorder. The day of the event all food is prepared and put into commercial carryout containers and bundled by order. Then set up your

curbside drive-thru stand/tables at the designated time and **whalaa, you have your drive-thru dinner**! Be sure all FOOD SAFE HANDLING TEMPS AND PROCEDURES ARE FOLLOWED!

5. **Silent Auctions**. These are auctions that are held without an auctioneer. You place donated items out on tables with a bid sheet and people are to place bids for a set amount of time. The time is usually 30-60 minutes depending on the event and number of donations. You and your group will collect donations such as meals, weekend get a-ways, gift certificates from local businesses, local area attractions, and gift baskets. You can also make the baskets from your donated items. Be creative, many of the small items will do better when bundled in a gift basket. Plan an event or a time after church when you can set up the auction. Make bid sheets, these can be as simple or as fancy as you would like them. Describe the item and starting bid of the item on each bid sheet. Number the bid sheet for the bidders. At the close of the bidding time, you want to announce all your winners and hand out the gifts. Be sure to send thank you notes and receipts for all your donations.

Prayer support is also crucial to your successful trip. Usually it is a handful of committed people praying for your short-term mission trip. It's better to have a few that have a real concern and burden than to ask hundreds of people that will quickly forget about praying for you. Be sure to be prepared to give your prayer warriors a report about your trip after returning home!

Donated supplies are also another way for people to contribute to your trip. These are supplies you will take with you on your trip to give to the community or use for your ministry. This list is also covered in the packing chapter. Each trip will be different since needs will be different. Here are some items that may be donated:

- Bibles and tracts
- Medical supplies, medicines and vitamins
- School supplies
- Flip flops
- Children's toys and clothes
- Dental supplies such as toothbrushes and toothpaste
- Construction tools and supplies

One of the participants of my survey said they take all of their VBS supplies such as balls, bubbles, sidewalk chalk, VBS stories, songs/crafts. They also like to take fun gifts for the community. They like to find things they can't get in their country and bless them.

Takeaways

- Start planning how you will finance your trip as early as possible. Check with your leader to see if the group will be doing fundraisers together. You will probably still be raising support and fundraising up until you go on your trip.
- Support comes from others, your savings, doing fundraisers and needed supplies.
- PRAYER

Section 3

Spiritual preparation and packing lists

Time frame is 2-6 months before your trip

Chapter 9
Prepare spiritually and culturally

AFTER YOU HAVE PRAYED and asked the Lord if you should go on this trip and after you have picked a trip, it's a good time to prepare spiritually and culturally. I found a government website that can be helpful concerning facts about your country. I will also list many mission books that will also help you prepare spiritually.

Let's start with the facts about the country. The CIA has a website for 267 world entities. You can find much information on a country's history, the people, their government, economy, geography, communications, transportation and their military. The website is http://cia.gov/library/publications-the-world-factbook. On this page there is a dropdown menu over on the top right. Use the dropdown menu to select your country. Click on your country and this will open a page with all of the above information. Click on the + signs for more about each topic. You can also learn more about world news and how it may affect your trip at state.gov to access the US Department of State. On that page, look for quick links. Click on quick links and then on "travel warnings". I'm not saying that if you see problems in that country you shouldn't go on your trip. The information is there if you want it.

How do we prepare culturally for a 2-week short-term mission trip? You will get varied responses from different people. It is a good idea to research the people of your country on Google. Read as much as you can about their history and culture. You can visit with missionaries from that country and possibly you can meet people from your country and spend time with them. These are all good things to do to increase your awareness.

Remember, it is good to prepare and learn, however, God may have different plans for us. Let's go forward with our plans and dreams, but we are truly only useful to God when we have total dependence on Him. So, even if we are well prepared and we go on a mission trip and we feel it is a failure, God can still use it for His glory. A word to all of us, prepare but GO with humble hearts to serve!

How do we prepare spiritually?

You more than likely will be joining a group to go on your trip. Your group may require you to read a missions book or do a missions devotional. They will probably have pre-trip meetings to prepare. Meetings are a good time to meet other trip members and go over the purpose and work projects of your trip. It can also be a good time to do group devotionals and prayer. Most of the groups do get together once a week for the last six to eight weeks before the trip.

You don't need to wait for your group to start preparing spiritually. Start praying for your trip as soon as you decide. Here's a prayer list you may want to use:

- Pray for the trip, the team and yourself.

- Pray for your host church or mission organization in the host country.

- Pray for favor and protection while traveling. Pray for good interpreters, team cooperation and servant hearts.

- And anything else!

There are books and Bible studies that can help you prepare for your trip. I would start reading six to nine months before your trip or as soon as possible. Some of these books I have read to prepare for trips or for writing this book. Other books were recommended by the participants in my survey. The participants are either mission group leaders or missionaries. I really appreciate their help and input.

I will list the books here. If you would like to share with me about any of the books, you can email me at: travel55plus@gmail.com. All of the books can be purchased on Amazon for around $10.

1. *Helping without Hurting in Short-term Missions* - by Steve Corbett
This book helps us to realize that we aren't always helping when we go on mission trips. This book helps us to understand how and why we should go on trips and how to make a difference. They also have a small group study for 6 weeks.

2. *Serving with Eyes Wide* Open: *Doing Short Term Missions with Cultural Intelligence* - by David A Livermore
This book helps us to rethink our mission trips. Why are we traveling to another continent to paint walls? This book helps us to grow our knowledge of other cultures and build relationships. We can help with manual labor, but what else can we do?

3. *Unlocking Mission and Eschatology in Youth Ministry* - by Andrew Root
Even though written for youth ministry, it can be helpful to all of us. The book is written in story form and easy to understand.

The definition of eschatology is the part of theology concerned with death, judgment, and the final destiny of the soul and of humankind.

4. *A Hole in the Gospel* – by Richard Stearns
This is the story of how God called Richard to be president

of World Vision. I want to share what it says on the back cover.

"What does God expect of us? Is our faith just about going to church, studying the Bible and avoiding the most serious sins? Or does God expect more? Have we embraced the whole gospel or a gospel with a hole in it?"

5. *Radical Together* - by David Platt
This book encourages Christians to join together as the "church" instead of being a bunch of individuals. It is helping us learn to live out our faith in practical ways and short-term mission is one of those ways.

6. *How to Plan, Prepare and Successfully Complete your Short-Term Mission* - by Matthew Backholer
This is a pretty big book with a lot of good and practical information for STM's. I did learn a lot from it, however, I felt the material wasn't well organized.

Here is a list of books, devotionals, Bible studies and a course that are suggested from the people in my surveys. One of the questions asked was what they did to prepare and what books they used.

1. *Short-Term Missions Workbook: From Mission Tourists to Global Citizens* by Tim Dearborn

This is an 8 weeks course for teams to do together. You can purchase this on Christianbook.com.

2. *Six Short-term trip Non-Negotiables* - This is a 2 page list of the 6 things we need to remember on trips. I will print this at the end of this chapter. #1 and #2 were shared by Kelly Argot from Daybreak Church in Mechanicsburg, PA

3. *Before you Go: Forty Days of Preparation for a STM.* A Daily Devotional by Jack Hempfling

This is a 40-day journal to do with your team before going on your trip. It helps with everything from finances to getting your hearts ready to serve. This can also be found on Christianbook.com

4. **Perspectives course**

This is a 15-week course designed around 4 perspectives about mission. The four perspectives are Biblical, Historical, Cultural and Strategic. Each of these highlights different aspects of God's global purpose. You can either take the class in select cities or take it online. For more information visit their website at www.perspectives.org. #3 and #4 were shared by Pastor Steve Newman from First Baptist Church of Lodi, Lodi, CA.

5. *The Next Christendom: The Coming of Global Christianity* by Philip Jenkins

6. *A Common Mission: Healthy Patterns in Congregational Mission Partnerships* by David Wesley

7. *Toxic Charity: How Churches and Charities Hurt those they Help(and how to reverse it)* by Patrick Lawlor and Robert Lupton

8. *Short-Term Mission: An Ethnography of Christian Travel Narrative and Experience* by Brian M Howell

The definition of Ethnography: The scientific description of the customs of individual peoples and cultures.

9. *The Celtic Way of Evangelism: How Christianity can reach the West...Again* by George G Hunter III

Items #5 - #9 were all recommended by my son, Ryan Albaugh. He's associate pastor at Mesa First Church of the Nazarene in Mesa, AZ.

You can buy any of these books from Amazon.

Another great resource is **On the Red Box**. You can access this on the internet at eng.ontheredbox.com. This is a ministry of my friends, Jacob and Julie Bock. They are full time missionaries to Spain since the 1980's. Julie and I have been friends since we were kids and now her and her husband have been faithfully sharing Christ in Spain for over 30 years!

Since 2002 they have been passing out tracts and preaching on the red box in downtown Madrid in the main plaza, the Puerto de Sol. They have seen God work in many lives. Now they have a training center near the square so they can train others to be evangelists. Please visit their website, eng.ontheredbox.com and see what God is doing in Spain and many other countries that are also using "On the Red Box" to reach the lost.

I would suggest joining the "Network" for free and you will have access to many more free resources. After you sign up you can click on "downloads" and then click ebooks. You will see many great ebooks listed. I have read Wonderful Plan and Aim for the Heart so far. I am planning to read many more.

They also have an ebook about giving your testimony. While you are on your mission trip and you go to the local church, you may be asked to give your testimony. This ebook is a good way to be prepared! Under testimony, click on "Preparing your testimony". This is only eight pages but a lot of information. They also have an easy to use outline to help you prepare. This is a one- page download where you can fill in the information asked for and use this to guide you while giving your testimony. These ebooks are an excellent source for preparation for your trip. Try to read as many as possible.

Kelly Argot from Daybreak Church shared a 2-page handout. The handout below does refer to Daybreak Church which you could easily change to your church or group.

<u>Six Short-term Trip Non-Negotiables</u>

1. Be a servant!

- Actively discovering and meeting the needs of someone else, above your own preferences
- Being flexible, regardless of what you came prepared to do
- Making yourself available to the International Workers (IW's) and the national church leaders, or partnering church/organization to do the "nobody wants to do them" jobs.

2. Go prepared!

- Servanthood starts by being prepared for your trip.
- Be prepared before you go and be responsible to your team for their preparedness.
- Be sure to work carefully through the training materials, and commit to investing all of the time, talent, and resources you need to lead a prepared team.

3. Lead as a team player!

- Four different groups of people to partner with to lead an effective short-term team:

    1. <u>**Daybreak's Global Ministries Team**</u> – The Global Ministries Team is here to equip and serve you in any way possible!
    2. <u>**Your teammates**</u> – You need the gifts and abilities of the whole team.
        - Model humility by delegating certain responsibilities to other team members.
        - Verbally affirm your team, individually and the team as a whole.

- Most importantly, lead by example – don't expect the team to do things you're not willing to do.

3. **The International Workers** – The IW's with whom you are going to serve know what is best.
    - Follow their lead on everything.
    - Serve without selfish questioning, always being willing to do whatever they ask.

4. **Partnering teams from other churches** – Your team may not be the only short-term team on the field.
    - Make choices that consider them first, even above the needs of your own team.
    - Find opportunities to encourage and affirm them.

4. Submit to Field Authority

Here are a few reasons why you should always submit to the leadership of the IW's (or partnering church/organization).

- They have been on the field much longer than you.
- They know the culture much better than you.
- They have influence in the community that you don't have and know how to best serve them.
- They know where God has already worked, where He is working now, and where He is moving in the near future.
- They know when something (though seemingly good to us) would be an inappropriate action or gift.

A few examples of submitting to an IW's leadership:

- If the IW asks you to do something during a time when you had already planned to hold a team meeting or take a nap or shower, cancel your plans and follow their request.
- If you come prepared to lead VBS, and the IW says they need to now cancel VBS, you graciously accept the cancellation, offer to give all of your supplies to the local church, and joyfully ask how else you may serve instead.

5. Practice sensitivity to the host culture!

Refer to your IW who is the expert on the culture's customs.
Ask them questions before you go, as well as when you arrive.
No question is too silly!
Here are a few examples:

- Learn how to greet others. (Are there gender specific rules?)
- Stay away from cultural "no-no's" (e.g. In Mali, don't shake, eat or do anything with your left hand.)
- Know how to dress appropriately in different settings.
- Ask about appropriate giving and/or tipping.
- Eat the food – give everything a shot! Don't offend your host cooks by not eating what they have prepared and probably sacrificed to make for you.
- Try the language – learn how to say some of the basics in your new language.

6. Follow the promptings of the Holy Spirit!

Trust God's voice! As a leader, God will speak things to you that He will choose to not speak to the rest of the team, except through you! Here are a few things for you to consider:

- Wake up each morning and ask God, "What are You saying to me today? Is there something You have planned for our team that you want to tell me about? Please give me eyes to see and ears to hear what you are doing." Pray this same prayer throughout the day, not just in the morning.
- Be willing to change your plans (under the leadership of the IW's, of course!) at any time, trusting that God's plans for each day are perfect.
- Expect to hear from God in new ways!

I'm including another 5-page article I think you will enjoy and find helpful.

When the Elephant Dances, the Mouse May Die <u>-The Dangers of Short-Term Missions</u>
By Miriam Adeney

"Let me tell you a story about Americans," an African Christian friend said to me. Elephant and Mouse were best friends. One day Elephant said, "Mouse, let's have a party!" Animals gathered from far and near. They ate. They drank. They sang. And they danced. And nobody celebrated more and danced harder than Elephant. After the party was over, Elephant exclaimed, "Mouse, did you ever go to a better party? What a blast!" But Mouse did not answer. "Mouse, where are you?" Elephant called. He looked around for his friend, and then shrank back in horror. There at Elephant's feet lay Mouse. His little body was ground into the dirt. He had been smashed by the big feet of his exuberant friend, Elephant. "Sometimes, that is what it is like to do mission with you Americans," the African storyteller commented. "It is like dancing with an Elephant.

We can hurt people through missions. The heartbeat of Christian living is in mission. The love of Christ propels us out of our comfort zones. Blessed spiritually and materially, we Americans owe a debt to the world. So, we go out in mission. As we go, we bring our strengths. An efficient, pragmatic, problem solving can-do-attitude. An egalitarianism. A vitality. Significant resources of all kinds. Yet we can hurt the people we go to with what we bring. When medicine is practiced poorly, when engineering is done badly, when cooking is unsanitary, people can get hurt. Despite well intentioned efforts, patients can die, bridges can collapse, and families can get sick. In the same way, short-term mission efforts done poorly can cause damage, sometimes great damage.

Are we actually serving our American "idols?" By definition, short-term missions have only a short time in which to "show a profit," to achieve predefined goals. This can accentuate our American idols of speed, quantification, compartmentalization, money, achievement, and success. Projects become more important than people. The wells dug. Fifty people converted. Got to give the church back home a good report. Got to prove the time and expense was well worth it. To get the job done (on our time scale), imported technology becomes more important than contextualized methods. Individual drive becomes more important than respect for elders, for old courtesies, for taking time. We end up dancing like elephants. We dance hard, and we have big feet.

Whose needs are really served? Short-term missions, if they are used primarily to meet our own needs, become selfish, self-centered. We need to expand our worldviews, for example. We need to strengthen relationship among our church members. We need to stimulate giving to our church mission projects. To provide wholesome service activities for our youth and adults. We need to be sensitized to suffering. Yes, short-term missions trips can meet these needs. But, we must ask ourselves, do we have the right to use others to get our needs met? Mission is at the heart of life with God. Americans have much to give. But, those of us involved in short-term missions need to watch out for quick-fix approaches and self-serving agendas.

Principles for effective short-term ministry. Here are five principles that will help make your next short-term experience constructive, not damaging 1. Get a comprehensive overview of what Christians are doing already in your destination country. Then be prepared to adapt to those priorities. 2. As people going for a short-term, be connected to long-term projects. Be sure this is done at the invitation of the locals. 3. Nurture long-term relations between those who send, those who go, and those who receive. Make you're a multi-year and multi-level series of exchanges 4. Work with, or develop, local leaders.

Help build self-sustaining structures which progressively empower other leaders and other structures in the host country. 5. Train all the participants on short-term mission team thoroughly. Train, train, train.

Server in the context of national expertise. Let's take a look at how these principles can be applied. As an example, is construction your call? Before you take another team of builders overseas, help the people in your host country to organize so they can eventually run the building operation themselves. This may mean finding national Christians who are economists, or development specialists, or contractors to work with you. Look for experienced nationals who can consult on the project, including legal issues. Maybe you can help the local community set up a cooperative organization, working together while they gain experience. Maybe this will mean inviting an agency with expertise, such as World Vision, to partner with you. Eventually there will be a place for your team of short-term builders. But that may be months or even years down the road. If you go sooner, you may be meeting your own needs more than the needs of those you claim to serve.

Using local resources to meet local needs. People should feel empowered when you leave. This is the lasting results of a successful short-term mission trip. Your national hosts should feel more confident about using locally available resources to solve their own problems. Why? Because that is what you have modeled. Ask yourself: Can you operate peacefully without e-mail, a computer, or a fax? Without electricity or a car? If not, what do you model for people who MUST operate that way? Do you buy the resources for your projects locally, thereby supporting the national economy and affirming the use of indigenous materials? Do you keep within a budget that the indigenous agency could maintain? This applies to construction supplies. It applies also to office supplies and equipment, to medical supplies, and to teaching materials like books, videos and tapes. "That item just isn't available here," you may be told.

Yes, sometimes you will need to import material. But let that be the exception rather than the rule. First, check what resources local professionals use. One example is Anne Thomas who trains teachers of reading in a government program. Her work is in isolated provinces in Laos. Wherever she is, the first thing she must do is to make books. She does that using the silkscreen method, a local resource. Before you import material for a Christian children's camp, are you sure there is no church or mission among this ethnic group anywhere in the world that has produced material for them? In most languages, the Jesus video is available. Sooner or later these people are going to have to write Christian books, Sunday school materials, etc. What are you doing to encourage that creativity?

Perhaps we should go, first of all, for our own education. "My grandchild went on a short-term trips and came home a new person!" this happens so often that we start thinking, "If it costs a little minor imperialism to save our grandchildren, well, nothings perfect." A woman writes to me. "How else can my grandkids experience suffering?" After all, our young people—and our midlifers—and our seniors—actually, all of us whatever our stage in life—do need to go on pilgrimage. From Abraham, to the Aeneid, to the Apollo moon landing, the journey is a classic motif for growth. If we are honest with ourselves we will have to admit that a short-term mission trip is often primarily an educational experience in which we are the learners. That's good. But, a learner learns best out of humble spirit of non-interference. And that can conflict with our stated desire for active service. So a check on our motives may be in order. Do we need to be needed? Are we driven to solve problems? Must we provide a report of achievements for our donors? Such concerns can breed a subtle arrogance. By contrast, if we see short-term missions as education, we will be more ready to learn humbly. This need not preclude service, but it may well reorder the way we go about it.

Starting right here-at-home may be best. For all of us there may be another alternative we should explore first. Poverty suffering and cross-cultural color. Fiesta and friends. All are right across town. In my home city, Seattle, for example, ninety languages are spoken. For unskilled youth, in particular, this may be the place to start. Suppose an ethnic church and a main-culture church in the same city would exchange youth groups for the month of July, with the kids moving into each other's homes. Scary? A journey? Yes. The results would reverberate for decades in that city. A journey of ten thousands miles may begin on a local bus. This is not glamorous. We may prefer "Afghan-istanitis" that is serving exotic people in exotic places. How much more exciting (and how much more under our control) that overseas trip may be than befriending Mexicans across town. After all, who knows but what they might show up on our doorstep for an exchange visit! Yet when these local Mexicans or Afghans or Vietnamese commend us to their families in their distant homelands, we will be welcomed there for long-term mission rooted in relationships. In any case, what benefits us, or our grandchildren, is not the top priority. Mission is not therapy. Christ did no come primarily to enhance his own experience. He came to serve, and he started with what was near at hand.

Is some of it a waste of money? "Americans have to see it to support it." Is that really true? Yes, people give to people. But not everybody needs a video of themselves on the field. We just need to know somebody in the project. We need to feel that we are a vital part of the teams of sender, goers, and receivers. And, we need to be kept up to date personally. When it comes to financial support, American Christians aren't stupid. We can understand basic math. "I've gotten five letters in the past couple of weeks from friends who are going overseas on two-week trips. I wonder if the Lord's money couldn't be spent better?" confided by well-to-do friend Evelyn. "I mean I gave to each one. But from a financial point of view, I hate to take away from the people who are there from the long-term, and then have to come home for lack of resources." A "gotta-see-it-to-support-it" mentality simply lets too many Christians off the hook. Sometimes we seem to be saying "if you're really committed, go on a short-term trip. Otherwise, just go shopping at the mall." Is what we sometimes seem to be saying. But that split is perverse. Every Christian is called to care, and every Christian can find a place as a part of team concerned for global mission where personal relationships are vibrant.

Training that lasts. How well are your short-term team members trained? First, consider spiritual factors. Do they know the great themes of Scripture? Can they discuss "difficult questions" with non-Christians? Can they share their own stories? Can they help a new Christian grow? Are they faithful in their own personal practice of daily spiritual disciplines? Even the carpenter, the surgeon, and the "closed country" visitor—whose witnesses are largely "Christian presence"—need to be able to give an answer for the hope that is in them.

Well-prepared teams can witness in the most formidable places. I found such a team in Mauritania enjoying regular opportunities. But poorly prepared teams will let the chances of a lifetime slip through their fingers. I've met teams like that, too. Then consider the cultural knowledge and interpersonal skills that your team members need to be effective. Training in this area will include contextualized apologetics—ideas on how to express the Christian faith in terms of the local great religion, worldview, values, and felt needs. Team members also should know the history of the Church in the particular country to which they are going. And, don't forget practical details. Of the many short-term teams I have helped to train recently, at least two plans to house their members individually in local homes (in Brazil and Russia). I heartily recommend this where possible. But, this excellent strategy reminds us of the need for practical preparation.

Elephants who dance delicately. A few years ago, a group in a church in Oregon met to study and pray about missions. Up to this point there had been little mission interest in this church. The group recommended sending a short-term team to the Wolof of Senegal, a Muslim people, which the church did. This was an educational, get-acquainted trip. Back home again, the team reported on the Wolof's need for water. The church decided to raise a few thousand dollars for World Vision to dig wells. In due course, the wells were dug. The next years, a half dozen Senegalese villages invited the church to send a team to join with them in parties celebrating the water. After all, friendship means laughing together, as well as solving problems together.

On this second trip, not only did the team celebrate the water, but they also discovered an evangelist to the Wolof. This servant of God was sent out from a nearby people group. Now short-term teams from the Oregon church are working with this evangelist, in the context of a web of established friendships. My own church, University Presbyterian Church in Seattle, has been working in Albania since 1991. During the first five years of our work, 22 members from UPC gave a total of 57 years of service in that country. Some were long term (from a commitment of 2-5 years to a lifetime focused on Albanians). And, many others were short-term. All were needed. In Albania, all our people fitted into long term work that progressively empowered local leaders. In particular, we worked closely with a local evangelical church association and with a local university student ministry. Both began just seven years ago. Today both these networks run themselves. To sum up, connect short-term mission participants with long term projects. And not just any project but ones that are owned and run by indigenous Christians. Will it always go smoothly? Will it always be a piece of cake? No. Some indigenous Christians, like many here in American, are self-serving. Others are no well trained or gifted for the roles in which they are cast. Welcome to real life, at home or abroad!

In real life, in real world missions there is always risk. Ambiguity, the possibility of failure, different understandings of financial accountability and standards of excellence, the need for training—all these issues must be faced. There is no short cut. To give the members of our supporting churches the idea that mission is always simple, always convenient, always pure, and always successful does not jibe with Christian realities, or human realities. No friends are perfect. No program works fully, or forever. But love covers a multitude of sins. And when we have discovered fathers, mothers, brothers and sisters in another place through the work of the gospel, how rich that love can be.

— Mirian Adeney (Ph.D. Anthropology, M.A. Journalism) is Research Professor of Mission at Regent College, and Associate Professor of Global and Urban Ministries at Seattle Pacific University.

She has lived or worked in Micronesia, Philippians, Brazil, Mexico, a North American Indian reservation, Russia, Mali, Nepal, and Malaysia. One of her current interests is training Two-Thirds World Christian leaders to write books that are biblically rich and culturally contextualized. Another current focus is ministry to Muslim women.

Chapter 10
Make your packing and shopping lists

LET'S START WITH PREPARING for packing for our trip. Let's look at what we will need.

How do we pick the right bags/suitcases?

Pick a suitcase or large backpack for your clothes and personal hygiene items. If you are thinking of traveling with a large backpack, ask yourself if you can carry it on your back for at least one hour. If you are thinking of taking a suitcase, ask yourself if it will be a carry on and if you can lift it over your head into the bins on the plane.

It is recommended to take three bags on your trip.

1. A moderate size backpack or suitcase. Find a sturdy one since it will see many miles and be tossed around by baggage handlers.

2. A carryon bag to keep at your seat in the plane. This can be a medium size backpack or large tote.

3. Purse for women or bro bag for men. Some people may prefer to combine these items in with your backpack or tote. If you decide to not take the smaller bag, at least get a money belt or an underarm conceal pack for passports, money and credit cards.

Start making your shopping list. Do you need any of the above items?

Do you need a suitcase, backpack, tote, bro bag, money belt, underarm conceal pack?

Let's start our packing list for the two smaller bags that you'll take on the plane.

Example packing list for your medium size bag such as a backpack or tote bag.

1. Extra set of clothes in case your suitcase is lost.

2. Your prescription meds for your entire trip except the ones you need for traveling. You'll put those in your purse or bro bag.

3. Electronics such as laptop, ipad, or tablet. Pack their chargers also.

4. Travel adapters if they'll be needed in overseas airports to charge your electronics.

5. Toiletries. Toothbrush and toothpaste and anything else you would like to have with you. Would you like to have facial wipes? Remember, all liquids need to be in 4 oz. containers and in a zip lock bag.

6. Small jacket. Something you can roll up when not wearing.

7. Snacks. Don't get chocolate.

8. Empty reusable water bottle. Fill this after you pass security.

9. Small notebook and pens.

Example packing list for your smaller bag such as a purse or bro bag.

Messenger bags are good small traveling bags for men or women. They are sturdy and have shoulder straps. This is what I call the 'bro bag'. These can be purchased from Amazon. An example description of a men's bro bag is as follows:

"BroBag Men's vintage canvas messenger satchel shoulder military field bag". At the time of writing this, the price is $35.00.

1. Passport and your travel documents.

2. Wallet and money belt. Cash, debit and credit cards. Do you need to exchange some cash into the local currency before you leave or can you do it after arriving?

3. Prescription meds for your trip.

4. Cell phone and chargers.

5. Camera, batteries, chargers and memory cards.

6. Hand sanitizer, chap stick and lotion.

7. Anything else you need handy.

Money Exchange while overseas. If you use your credit card or debit card, the bank will automatically and accurately do the exchange rate for you. This is probably the easiest way to purchase items overseas. If you do need cash, you can also use your ATM card at their local bank and it will accurately exchange it for you. Some countries like Panama take US dollars. To find out if your visiting country takes US dollars, do a Google search, such as 'Does Costa Rica accept US dollars?' That's even easier!

Before we do the packing list for your suitcase or backpack, here is a suggested list of <u>what not to bring on a mission trip.</u>

1. Expensive jewelry including your diamond wedding ring.

2. Fancy clothes and purses.

3. Patriotic or military clothing.

4. Be modest. Don't bring low necklines or short shorts or skirts.

5. Maybe jeans, check with your leader.

6. Maybe shorts, check with your leader.

We want to go with humble hearts and we don't want to alienate people by taking our expensive things with us.

Example packing list for your suitcase or large backpack.

To check your bag at the airport, the weight limit is 50 lbs. You can use a handheld scale to weigh your bag before traveling. The overweight cost of a bag can be over $100.

1. Bible and journal. Have a journal handy to write down things God is teaching you.

2. Copies of your passport, Visa and Driver's License. Have a copy in your suitcase and leave a copy at home with your family. The originals keep with you in your small bag or money belt. Have a copy of your travel plans in your suitcase and leave a copy at home also.

3. Mosquito repellent and sunscreen. Mosquito repellent with Deet works best.

4. Spare glasses or contacts.

5. Small flashlight and batteries.

6. First Aid Kit. Ask your leader if the group is bringing one. If not, you may want to bring a few helpful items. These items may include alcohol swabs, antibacterial cream, gauze, tape and band aids, antihistamine for allergic reactions, cold medicine, diarrhea medicine and motion sickness pills.

7. Snacks for later in the trip. Nothing that will melt.

8. Small gift for your host. Again, check with your leader.

Example packing list of clothing.

You can adjust this list to meet your needs.

1. Church clothes. It is suggested that women wear long skirts and men wear a collar shirt and dress pants. This probably doesn't apply to all countries, but it does apply to most. If in doubt, ask your leader.

2. (2) every day pants or skirts.

3. (2) every day shirts or t-shirts.

4. (1) rain jacket or warmer coat for cold climate.

5. Underwear and socks

6. (1) pair of walking shoes and/or work boots

7. (1) wide brim hat or baseball cap

8. (1) set of sleepwear

9. (1) set of flip flops to wear for showers

10. For warmer weather: (1) pair of sport sandals, swim suit, (2) pairs of shorts or capris

Example packing list of gadgets

1. Cell phone. You can also use your cell phone as a flashlight and alarm clock. See next chapter, "Explore your Cell phone options" for information on how to get service and internet.

2. Electrical converter. Does your country require a 220 converter for your devices?

You can check online to see what voltage the country uses. It's best to do a Google search for "*Complete list: Plug, socket and voltage by country – World Standards*".

3. Camera. If you don't want to use your cell phone as your camera, be sure to remember batteries or battery charger and extra memory cards.

4. Rechargeable battery pack to charge your cell phone. Charge it up in your room at night and take it with you so you'll always have your phone charged. Bring (2) USB cords so you can charge your phone at night and your rechargeable battery pack.

5. Portable suitcase scale. We can't travel without our scale. This is very important to make sure your bag or suitcase isn't over 50 lbs. They charge you a lot for being overweight.

Example packing list for team materials/donations

Many mission teams take supplies with them for their host. Teams will ask each person to collect items needed and then bring an extra bag or suitcase to pack the items.

Items that may be needed include the following:

- Bibles and tracts, VBS supplies

- Medical supplies, medicines and vitamins

- Dental supplies including toothbrushes and toothpaste

- School supplies

- Flip flops

- Children's toys and clothes

- Construction tools and supplies

It is difficult for churches and ministries to mail these supplies to other countries. Many times they will get lost or stolen. Traveling with the goods does help but not always. They may still get lost or stolen.

Now it's time to make your shopping list. Go through all of the above packing lists to make your shopping list.

Section 4

Getting things done before leaving

Time Frame is last month before trip

Chapter 11
Explore your cell phone options

YOU WILL PROBABLY WANT to keep in touch with your family while you are gone, so we'll explore some options for using it while on your trip. What are your choices for phone calls, texts and using the internet?

1. You can use your cell phone carrier's international plan. These can be expensive. Some of the plans you can't really know how much it will cost for data and roaming until you get the bill. It's worth looking into it.

2. *Verizon's travel plan.* I use Verizon, so I wanted to see what they had for traveling. They offer a travel pass. At the time of writing this book, you can use your data/talk/text allowances in other countries for $10/day or $5/day for Mexico and Canada. You have the same plan that you would have at home but you are only charged for the days that you use your phone. You can sign up for this on the Verizon website or on their app.

3. You can call and text people for free with the free apps, *Whatsapp* and *Viber.* They use the internet instead of your phone's minutes. Remember you will be using your data and not your cell phone plan's minutes or texts. Make sure you have your family get either of these apps before you leave home. You can either use the Wi-Fi at a hotel, etc. or you can get a pocket Wi-Fi. These apps can be used on all the

latest model cell phones. You make phone calls just like you would when you are home. You can also share documents up to 100mb. It is easier than email.

4. *Wireless Traveler.com* has a global pocket Wi-Fi device and free Wi-Fi app. It has a few options to help you stay connected while traveling overseas. The 4 options include: Global pocket Wi-Fi device and Wi-Fi app, global sim card for your cell phone, purchase or rent a global cell phone for remote locations and you can also rent a satellite phone. They provide all the details on their website.

For most trips, the best choice will be the global pocket Wi-Fi device and their free Wi-Fi app. The pocket Wi-Fi will give you secure service while you are gone from your hotel or home base. You can connect to 5 devices to this pocket Wi-Fi which is a hotspot. So, while you are busy during the day you can access your emails, GPS, Internet or anything else that needs Wi-Fi. The app allows you to make and receive calls and texts free from other phones with the same app. If you are making or receiving calls from landlines or cell phones in the US, the rate is 2 cents a minute. You will also buy a data plan for your trip. For example, a two- week trip to Panama using the pocket Wi-Fi with 100 MB of data will cost you $73.

The breakdown of the cost is the pocket Wi-Fi rental for 2 weeks is $38 and the 100mb of data is $35 which equals $73. Plus, you would probably prepay $10 for minutes you will use calling landlines or cell phones. Remember app to app using Wi-Fi is free just like WhatsApp and Viber.

5. *Local sim cards.* You can go to the airport in your host country and buy a local sim card from a vending machine for your cell phone. Make sure your cell phone is unlocked before traveling. A major drawback to this is that you will receive a local phone number for that country and it's harder for people in the US to reach you. Many of the newer cell phones you can't put in a new sim card.

Chapter 12
Let's GET it done!

YOU'VE BEEN PREPARING for months. You have collected information on everything you need to know. You have your passport and your travel visa (if needed).

Let's go out and get all those things done.

1. Get your shots and medicines. See chapter 6

2. Get your travel health insurance and trip cancellation insurance. See chapter 6

3. Get your cell phone plan for overseas. See chapter 11

4. Get your shopping done for all your gadgets, clothes and toiletries.

See chapter 10

5. Get packed!

In Addition to the above, here's your check off list of the last 10 things to do before leaving home:

1. Exchange at your bank $50 so you have local money to spend when you arrive.

2. Notify all credit card companies and your bank that you will be traveling. They monitor use of your credit cards and your debit card and may decline purchases if not notified. Call the customer service number on the back of your cards.

3. Have your mail stopped. You can either go to the post office and fill out a "hold mail" form or you can call 800-275-8777 to schedule a vacation hold.

4. Write down all your medications with dosage and strength and keep a copy with you and one in your luggage.

5. Put copies of your passport and travel itinerary in your luggage.

6. Get your trip contact information from your leader and email it to your family and close friends. If you are taking your cell phone, let them know you will have it with you. Tell them about the free apps and if you are using WhatsApp, Viber or Wireless traveler. Encourage them to use the same one you are using so that calling and texting is free when using Wi-Fi. If not, make sure they have a way to contact you in case of an EMERGENCY at home while you are gone. If they can't reach you directly using the free Wi-Fi app, can they call your leader on their cell phone? Or does the visiting ministry have a US phone number? If they don't have a US number, do you have the international phone number? Who is the contact person for the ministry where you are going? Also, does your family at home know how to make an international phone call?

7. Arrange for paying your bills while gone. Mail them ahead or schedule them online.

8. Eat up as many of the perishables as possible in your refrigerator. Give away food if it will spoil while you are gone.

9. Go over your packing lists and make sure you have everything. DON'T FORGET YOUR PASSPORT!

10. Final check of your house. Make sure all windows and doors are locked. Computers are off. All automatic appliances like the coffee pot is off or unplugged. Turn off the hot water heater. Take out your last bit of trash.

GO ON YOUR TRIP! BE A BLESSING TO OTHERS!

Here are a few tips to surviving your long flight:

1. Have all your prescriptions with you in your purse or small bag. Make sure you have all your over the counter drugs like allergy meds and motion sickness meds. Take all your meds according to your normal schedule then you can adjust to your new time zone after you arrive at your destination.

2. Drink plenty of water. Use eye drops if needed. Keep your water bottle filled and near you. To help prevent bloating, you can take *Gas-X* and avoid carbonated drinks.

3. Try to exercise. In your seat you can flex your ankles and feet. Try to get up and walk up and down the aisles of the plane. Walk when you're waiting in the terminals. By doing some exercise you can help prevent blood clots in your legs and swelling in your feet and ankles.

4. Try and get enough sleep. That's a really tough one. Use a neck pillow and eye mask if they help. Some people can sleep on flights and others can't. You may want to take over the counter sleep aids.

5. Since you are 100 times more likely to catch a cold on a plane, try taking Airborne or other supplements to boost your immune system before your flight.

6. Adjust to the new time zone. The best way to adjust is when you land, try to stay awake as close as possible to your normal bed time. At least try to stay awake until after dinner. That will help you with jet lag.

Section 5 will be about your time on the ground and arriving back home from your mission trip. Be sure to read it before your trip since there are many more good tips!

Section 5

After arriving in your host country

and returning home

Chapter 13
How to be safe and minister

THIS CHAPTER WILL BE ABOUT when you are on your trip and you are in the host country. Let's say all your arrangements have been made for lodging and for transportation from the airport. What do you need to be aware of at your final destination?

Below are some basic guidelines for us while we are guests in another country.

1. Spend time in prayer.

2. Stay FLEXIBLE and have a good attitude – Don't go with god complexes but go with humbleness. We all have a mutual need for Christ in our lives!

3. Build relationships with fellow Christians. God can create opportunities for transformation in their lives and ours.

4. Never quit or you may miss out on blessings and life lessons.

5. Always be respectful to your host while you are with them. If they are providing you with lodging, here are some practical ways you can show them respect.

   a. Keep your room clean

b. Report any issues with your room to leaders. Such as anything broken.

c. Do anything asked of you as unto the Lord. Col 3:23 and I Cor 10:31.

d. Remember the pastor's name and those that are helping you.

Safety is also another great concern of ours while traveling. Here are a couple of good tips. Be aware of your surroundings and don't wander off alone. Be aware of locals at the airport and at your location. Don't let fear paralyze you. Here are a few common things that can happen to foreigners while on a short-term mission trip.

1. People may come up to you and appear to be friendly. They may want to show you something and have you follow them to a dark alley or a back room somewhere. They may rob you or cause you harm. Listen to your host about where it is safe to go.

2. Be aware of people bumping into you on the street because they may be pick pocketers. Keep your money and passport safe with a money belt or under arm wallet. If they're in a purse, keep it close to your body.

3. If you are witnessing on the street, and you invite a person to a nearby café for coffee, make yourself very clear. Many times, they think you are also buying them a meal.

4. If you are asking local people for directions to a restaurant or any place, that person will probably expect compensation for their help.

5. Money exchanges aren't always honest. Ask your host for a reputable exchange. A better alternative is to use an ATM so the exchange rate is correct. Don't use the internet for banking at public cafes to access your accounts, as they may not be secure.

Here are some common-sense safety tips while on your trip.

- Never go out alone. Stay together with your group and you shouldn't have any problems. Your group should try to travel by car at night instead of walking.

- Let others know where you are going.

- Avoid unsafe and war areas.

- Men should keep their money and passport inside a coat pocket or in a money belt inside the waist of their pants or in an underarm wallet.

- Women should carry a crossover handbag with a wide strap. Messenger bags usually have these kinds of straps. Keep it zipped and in front of you. Women can also use money belts or under arm wallets.

- Avoid wearing flashy jewelry. Keep it at home during a mission trip.

- Keep your cell phone and camera close to you. Try to not get distracted while taking photos.

- While out in public, don't put anything down unless someone is watching it for you.

Another safety issue is Water and Food.

Tips for water safety include:

- Drinking water is safe in North America, Europe, Australia and New Zealand.

- All other places use either boiled water, filtered or bottled water. Make sure you use clean water for brushing your teeth and washing your face. Don't take ice cubes unless you know they're safe.

- Soda is safe everywhere.

Tips for food safety include:

- The biggest risk for getting sick from the food is the bacteria on the surface of the food and from warm dishes sitting out too long and the bacteria multiplies.

- Ideal foods to eat while gone are:
    - Ones cooked quickly at high temperature and then served quickly
    - Food in cans or sealed packs
    - Fruit that can be peeled, like bananas
- Foods to avoid while gone are:
    - Salads and fresh fruits that will be washed under running water
    - Raw food or undercooked food
    - Raw seafood
    - Eggs
    - Unpasteurized dairy products

During our trip we will also experience another culture. There were suggestions for learning about your country's culture in the Spiritual Prep chapter. Now we are going to discuss it here since everywhere you go, there will be different cultures. What is culture? The definition of culture is the norm of life and the way things are done. That's why each group of people from every nation thinks the way they think is right and best. Or they think they are right because things have always been done that way. They may never stop to think of any other options. Sometimes, their traditions are just too strong to break.

Culture shock and fatigue sets in when people traveling to other countries have a sensory overload of all the differences between the US and the host country. This won't happen as often on one to two week short-term mission trips. If you do feel overwhelmed with all the differences, be sure to talk to your leader or teammates. Remind yourself why you are on the trip. Don't take to social media to complain. Get plenty of rest and food and water. Most importantly, ask God for His grace and wisdom.

Please remember that our Christian culture may also be different than their Christian culture. We don't want to export our style of Christianity. Try to be culturally sensitive to the local Christians. Some of the differences between us may include:

1. Some can't wear crosses.

2. Some can't have pierced ears or other piercings.

3. Some can't have tattoos

In some countries, these could be considered sins. Understanding other cultures is complex. We try not to enter into another culture to judge or condemn them but to serve them and reveal the love of Christ. We can do this by our words, lives and actions. We can't expect them to enter into our world when we are in their world. Always remember our culture is also full of flaws and weaknesses.

Let's be aware of other cultures do's and don'ts.

1. Don't stress out about being perfect. They understand we don't have the same culture.

2. Don't speak the gospel with Western lingo.

3. Don't brag about your material things back home.

4. Be sensitive about their dogs or other animals. Our dogs are mostly for pets and most of theirs are work animals.

As we go to serve, let's not just be moved by emotions. Let's try to stay on our purpose of going. Let's stay on task at hand. Don't let your surroundings make you stray from your purpose of spreading the gospel. You will see weird, wicked and much inequality. Keep praying and seeking God's purpose for your trip. Don't allow superiority, pride and prejudice to creep into your hearts. We are all made in God's image and need to hear the good news!

Let's look at the 'Big Picture' as we travel to other countries to serve. Let's look at the long-term growth potential for us and those we are visiting. Don't force 'something' special to happen. Go with the flow and allow God to work. If we go and have fellowship with other believers and we trust God, He will show up and do His work.

As we go and help others, let's be sensitive to those around us and treat them all with respect. In the US, we love to share our experiences on Facebook, Instagram etc. We love to take pictures everywhere we go. That's all good, but let's think of the people that live in that country. Are we really treating them with respect when we are constantly taking pictures and posting them on social media? Here are a couple of guidelines while on a trip:

1. Don't take pictures of conversations, people in a church service or in their homes. If you do, please ask for permission.

2. Don't take pictures of children without permission.

3. Some trips ban people from posting on social media while gone. If it's not banned, try to only post while off duty for the day. Discuss what you want to post with your teammates to be sure they will be respectful.

How do you process all that you have learned and all that you have done?   Usually most groups will have group devotionals at night to allow you to share your experiences of the day. It's a good idea to keep a simple journal. At the end of the day, jot down how your day went, the best part of your day and the most difficult thing of the day. Then 1-2 sentences explaining what the Lord taught you. It's good to have your journal when you return home and the trip seems like a blur.

How should we give to others while in another country? You will probably have many people coming up to you asking for assistance. There will probably be many good requests and we do want to help. It is best to let the local ministry or mission organization screen the requests and give as they see appropriate.

You will have many people around you helping you while you are serving in their country. These people will include interpreters, cooks and drivers. As a group, it is important to be a blessing give them money for helping you. I don't know if every group does this or not, but I'm pretty sure they do something special for them.

Ministering in other countries

How do we prepare for our work projects? Some projects, such as building projects may take weeks or months to get supplies to your site. This may not concern you as a participant and not the leader, but it's good to be aware of the process. So, you will want to pick a mission trip that won't deprive the locals of jobs because of you going. But we can partner with them. Maybe we have skills that they don't have or maybe we can work together. We always want to remember that going on a short-term mission trip is to be a blessing to others and sharing the love of Christ. This should be done through everything we do, including our building projects.

How do we prepare to evangelize? Always follow the lead of your group leader and host. We do want to make our trip about evangelism and help with humanitarian needs. Jesus does command us in Matthew 25:35-40 that we are to take care of the weak, sick and poor. So, we must be about the physical and spiritual needs of others.

Here are two things to remember while evangelizing in other places.

1. In some countries, the locals may be persecuted for you evangelizing. Always coordinate your efforts with your group or local ministry.

2. Don't necessarily preach your doctrine from your denomination. Try to keep it basic and blend in with the local ministry.

3. Be prepared to participate in their church services. You didn't only go there to do your project, but you went there

to minister. If you can preach or sing, you may be asked to share during a service. If you're not prepared to do either of those, be prepared to give your testimony. Every one of us has a testimony. You can get information on sharing your testimony at: *ontheredbox.org* under e-books.

Remember when you go to a different country, many things will be different from home. Don't get frustrated if the pastor is an hour late for church or that you didn't finish painting the walls for them. Try to make your trip more about building relationships and not about doing things our way, the American way! Most of the world values relationships over productivity. Let's go and make a difference. Allow the Lord to work in your life and their lives.

Chapter 14
Saying good-bye, debriefing and returning home

AT THE END OF YOUR 1-2 week short-term mission trip, there should be a debriefing meeting. You can do this before you leave or back home. This meeting should include everyone on the team. This is an opportunity to try and adjust back to a normal life as you return home. This should be a time for each member of the team to share their thoughts, highlights of the trip, their disappointments and what they have learned.

You also will be preparing to leave and say good-bye to all your new friends. Of course, please clean up after yourself and leave your room cleaner than you found it. Tell everyone thank you that helped make the trip possible. If you brought small gifts, be sure to give them away. The people you want to thank include: the team leader, pastor or host, the interpreter, guide, driver and cook. Be sure to say good-bye and gather e-mail addresses of those you want to keep in touch. If you brought donations, make sure they are all distributed to the right places and people.

Back home

Ultimately, we need to allow the Lord to use this trip to change us and how we live life and think about missions. The experience of going on a mission trip will be with us for a very long time. At the end of the trip, it will be about how we allow

God to help us grow for the long term. You may have heard all these stories about God working when they went on a mission trip. What if you go on a trip and don't have any stories to tell? What if everything went as planned? That is still awesome. Take away the positive from the experience. We all invest a lot of money into our short-term mission trips. We can easily spend $1,500 per week to go on these trips. Make the investment count. Allow the Lord to change our hearts.

Here's what long term engagement in missions may look like:

1. You will be more consistent in praying for missionaries and the ministries that support them.

2. You will become an advocate for those serving as missionaries. Especially the ones you visited. You will be able to tell their story. Try to stay connected with them via e-mail and newsletters.

3. You will be more willing to financially support missionaries. If you just commit to helping the ministry you visited, that will enable them to reach more people for Christ in their communities.

Those are only three potential ways that your trip can help you grow and make a difference when you return home. I'm sure you can think of many more.

There can also be stumbling blocks once you return. Stay humble and in prayer in order to avoid the following:

1. You put this experience behind you and thought of it as a one-time emotional high.

2. You enjoyed the traveling and you never really changed your daily life.

3. You became prideful and allowed yourself to think you were superior to others.

Allow the experience to change you for the better. A couple of ways you can change your daily life is to dig deeper into God's word and encourage and support missionaries. You can add to the above items as God shows you how the experience can help you grow.

I found a blog post from Team.org. The blog post explains why it's important to have a debriefing plan. The plan includes the following:

1. Share your experience with others.

2. Keep your zeal for missions fresh.

3. Continue growing.

4. Reconnect with your home church.

5. Lean into the Lord.

You can read the whole blog post at: www.team.org/blog/debrief-your-short-term-mission-trip/ This is written by Brianna Langley.

Team.org gave me permission to share this blog post and their site. They have many other helpful posts you may want to read.

I want to share what one church does for debriefing after a trip. This information comes from one of my surveys from Kelly Argot of Daybreak Church in PA. Her church has 2 debriefing meetings after their trip. The team leader encourages the team members to continue on with whatever God was speaking to them during the trip. They also discuss any issues bothering them when they return home (reverse culture shock). Some of the things the Lord has prompted them to do include: give more time, treasure or talent to further God's Kingdom. Some of the members go and serve again on a short-term mission trip or some have been called to serve full time on the mission field.

Section 6

Answers from surveys

Chapter 15
What others are saying

I WANTED TO FIND OUT what churches are doing for short-term mission trips and I wanted to find out for myself if long term missionaries actually want short-term missions to come and help them. So, I decided to write a few questions for a survey for short-term mission trip leaders at churches and for long term missionaries.

It wasn't a scientific survey. I contacted people I know, and I called a few random churches selected from the internet. I asked a friend of mine, Marissa Young if she could help me with the surveys. Marissa graduated from Simpson University and has served as a missionary in Ecuador, so I knew she also had people she could contact to help. Altogether 20 surveys were returned with very helpful information. The surveys either came from leaders at churches for short-term mission trips or from missionaries that are currently serving or have served as full time missionaries. I'll start with the questions and answers from the mission trip leaders.

1. How far in advance do you start planning a short-term mission trip?

I received answers that ranged anywhere from six months to two years. The trip that took two years was a youth trip to the Czech Republic.

2.   How do you choose your trip locations and ministries to help? For example, do you use your denomination to find a trip? Or do you use a national mission organization?   Or do you already have relationships with missionaries on the field?

These answers were pretty split between the three options.

3. What kinds of projects do you do when you go on a trip? Humanitarian? Building projects? Or is it faith building such as teaching pastors to preach or doing VBS for the children?

This answer included a little bit of everything. Many of the surveys mentioned wanting to meet the needs of the people. Here's a list of all the projects: they help at orphanages, building projects, church planting, Vacation Bible School and Bible teaching, disaster relief and encouragement to missionaries.

4. Do you ever take trips to encourage your fellow Christians to stay strong in their faith and you don't do work projects?

They all said that is part of every trip. Some of the churches do send people to encourage the missionaries' wives or to relieve the local pastor so he can get a break. Most all of them said relationship building is important every trip.

5. How do you make your travel arrangements? Do you research on the internet for the best deal or do you use a travel agency or does the mission organization plan it for you?

I had one response saying the mission organization plans it for them. I had a couple answers saying each person on the trip found their own travel. Then it was about 50/50 for groups researching and buying on the internet and using a travel agency. Almost everyone used their host for transportation to and from the airport.

6. Does your mission team purchase trip cancellation or travel health insurance for your trip?

About half said yes and half said no. One church does make it available.

I want to share one response from Kelly Argot from Daybreak Church in PA. Kelly writes, "We do get cancel for any reason travel insurance which we began doing about eight to nine years ago after our trip to Africa had to be postponed and rescheduled due to the safety in the area at that time."

7. How do you fundraise or raise support?

There were many different answers to this question. Here are the answers:

- Work projects, support letters, yard sales, donations, entertainment such as talent shows and movies, dinners, car washes and people used their savings.

8. What do your groups read or do for devotionals before and after the trip?

The books and devotionals they use and recommend are listed in the spiritual prep chapter.

I'd like to share another answer from the survey from Randy Fields from New Covenant Baptist Church in Grass Valley, CA. Randy said, "We meet a minimum of once a month preparing testimonies, doing Bible study together, praying together, skyping with our missionary, fundraising, balloon animal training, evangecube training and team building activities."

Here are a few other suggestions before going on a trip. Learn about the country's history, its culture and its current issues. Also, it's good to read a missions' book that discusses how to act cross-culturally and what the expectations are for a member of the missions' team representing Christians, the Church and Americans. That response came from Ryan Albaugh from Mesa First Church of the Nazarene, Mesa, AZ.

It looks different for every group, but it is important to prepare!

9. What advice or tips would you give groups when planning a trip?

Here are a few of the answers:

- Have a humble heart and be flexible. Try to make sure you have a heart for the trip.

- Talk to your group and include them in decisions being made during the trip so they don't get frustrated and the trip becomes stressful.

- Taking the gospel of Christ outside of our comfort zone is life changing, but we must be flexible.

- Go to serve the full-time missionaries. Try to keep in touch with them to encourage them. This helps to keep Western culture out of short-term missions.

- Make your trip about "relationships".

I would like to share one of the responses from Jim Bailey from The Stirring in Redding, CA. Jim told us that one of the most important things is to do the work ahead of time in order to put together a team that can do helpful and do effective things. Teams need to think and plan ahead to really make an impact on the trip and meet needs well. Jim wants those who have been served to say, "We love that team and want them to come back!" That is important in order to build and form great connections and relationships.

Here's another response from Ryan Albaugh from Mesa First Church of the Nazarene.

He says to try and not only take only strong Christians. Try to open the trip up to whoever wants to go. The goal is to minister and sometimes that means the people on the team.

10. What kind of donations or supplies do you take with you?

There is also a wide variety of items teams take with them. They include: flip flops, clothes, small toys, toothbrushes and toothpaste, fluoride, flannel blankets, small tools, school supplies, Tylenol and vitamins.

One of the responses was to not give money to individuals, only to leaders and they'll decide where it's needed. As you can see, we can all learn a lot from others that are going on trips. This is a lot of information that can help us make our trips even better!

As we listen to what long-term missionaries have to say about short-term mission trips, I want to share the verse, Acts 20:24

"However, I consider my life worth nothing to me; my only aim is to finish the race and complete the task of testifying to the good news of God's grace."

That verse describes our long-term missionaries. They give up much to proclaim the gospel. The US has the privilege to send Christian missionaries all over the world. They leave home and all their comforts to take the gospel to the ends of the earth. With the help of my friend, Marissa Young, we were able to hear what they think about short-term mission trips. Here are the 4 questions.

Number 1 question of the survey. Do you think it's important for churches in the US to send short-term mission trips overseas? Why or why not?

They all said yes that short-term mission trips are important. Here are their reasons.

> 1. Trips help Americans experience the broader world outside the US.
>
> 2. Trips become a classroom where God meets and challenges all of us. God opens our minds to more aspects of Him and helps us grow as Christians.
>
> 3. Many long-term missionaries are called to full time service after being on a short-term trip.
>
> 4. People on a trip are a great encouragement to local believers and leaders as well as the missionary.

The missionaries also shared what not to do on a trip.

> 1. Don't be a know it all. Listen to advice of the full-time missionary.
>
> 2. Don't go to be served and entertained.

3. Don't bring a bunch of people to do things they don't do at home. A good example is construction projects. Many times, the locals tear down what the team did and hire their local professionals. Please bring qualified people if you will be doing construction.

Number 2 question of the survey. What do you think is the most important role for the teams that come to help? For example, should it be to encourage local believers? Or do building projects? Or do community projects like digging water wells?

Here are their answers.

1. Do what is needed and be a servant.

2. Evangelism. It's important whenever possible to do the most direct mission which is evangelism.

3. People should learn about the history and culture so they know better how to teach and lead the people of a different country.

4. Encourage and support local Christians and the full-time missionaries.

5. Construction, if needed and take professionals with you.

I want to share two of the answers from my survey. The first one is from Julie Bock who has been a missionary to Spain for over 30 years. Jacob and Julie do proclamation evangelism in downtown Madrid in the main square where over 120,000 people pass by every day. They go out on the square, step up on a box and proclaim how Jesus changed their lives and invite everyone to start following Jesus.

Julie's answer to this question, "Team members are more prepared for evangelism than they think. They already have the most important ingredient. They walk with Jesus. Therefore, they can share their story about Jesus changing their lives and forgiving them. Then they can share the simple story of Jesus' death and resurrection. POWERFUL."

The second answer is from Rich and Elisa Brown. They have been missionaries since 1994 in Peru and Ecuador. They started the ministry Inca Link in 2006 in order to reach 300 million youth in Latin America. Currently they have 18 missionaries and 90 nationals in 3 countries, Peru, Ecuador and Columbia. Their goal is to spread Inca Link to 16 new countries in 16 years.

Rich and Elisa's answer to this question. Remember the question is asking what is most important role for the teams. They say, "We see 4 main groups of people that MUST be blessed for it to work well."

> a. The ones with the suitcases coming down. They have got to be challenged and return to produce fruit for the Kingdom back home.

> b. The church that sends them – and the people that they get support. A testimony or new ministry, an opportunity that they didn't have before can happen as the church sees their own people come back changed for God.

> c. The church on the ground on the mission field as the team serves and provides resources for the church building, the orphanage, the pastors, the missionaries, etc.

> d. The community where the church is on the mission field. These people need to see our teams serving as Christ would serve. Sweeping the streets, sharing a smile, donating items to their kids, etc.

They end it with, "ALL is IMPORTANT".

I also received answers saying what we shouldn't be doing.

> 1. Don't go with an agenda other than to be a servant.

2. Don't assume a culture/people will understand all the Christian principles that we would in our churches.

Number 3 question of the survey. Have you ever hosted a short-term mission group while you were on the mission field? If so, how did they help you? How much time did it take you to prepare for their arrival and how much time did it take you to clean up after their departure? Will you host groups again? How would you change what you did?

A summary of what they said is that having teams is important. But, when missionaries are new to the mission field, it usually takes a lot of time to plan for and host teams. Some things they have learned along the way:

1. Have projects ready for the teams.

2. Have teams arrange their own meals.

3. Set up an orientation time to go over the plans.

4. Missionaries would like us to come help, but surrender our ideas and expectations and see what God can do.

5. They have learned they need to take care of themselves and not have so many teams coming that they are exhausted.

Overall, they were committed to hosting teams again. I would like to share Rich and Elisa Brown's answer. They say, "We've hosted about 150 teams over the past 15 years. We spent a lot of time to prepare in the early years. Now it's probably about 3 days.

We have interns, other missionaries to help share the load both before and after the team comes. Yes, we will continue doing it as we see the value for the Kingdom as a whole. Us, them, the nationals, the church in both countries and the Kingdom grows through this." I thought that was a perfect answer. It's important to ALL of us.

Number 4 question of the survey. Do you think it is important to have participants that are age 55 and over? In what ways do/would they benefit your ministry?

Here are their answers.

1. They offer love and support for the missionaries.

2. Older people are often better at comforting, listening and making people feel at ease with sharing their needs and their stories.

3. They offer expertise in many fields such as construction, teaching and medical.

4. They understand the value of working alongside missionaries and Christians from other countries.

They did mention two things that could be a hindrance when bringing older team members.

1. Sometimes they get an attitude because of their experience.

2. Some people go that shouldn't because of their health is-sues.

Overall, I believe God can use us that are older than 55. We have much to offer. Thanks again to all of the participants in the survey. I really appreciate their time and thoughtful answers. I hope and pray that you are inspired to go on a short-term mission trip or help support others that do. Remember, we can also make a difference by walking across the street to our neighbor. Wherever you go and whatever you do, may God richly bless you and use you for His Kingdom.

I want to thank all the participants in my survey.

The following are the mission trip leaders:

1. Jim Bailey - The Stirring, Redding, CA

 thestirring.org

2. Debra Strombeck - The Heights Church, Prescott, AZ

heightschurch.com

3. Stephen Newman - First Baptist Church, Lodi, CA

fbclodi.org

4. Ryan Albaugh - Mesa First Church of the Nazarene, Mesa, AZ

mesanaz.org

5. Randy Fields - New Covenant Baptist Church, Grass Valley, AZ

newcovenantbaptistchurch.org

6. Mark Becker - Shasta Baptist Church, Redding, CA

shastabaptistchurch.com

7. Kelly Argot - Daybreak Church, Mechanicsburg, PA

daybreakweb.com

8. Gordon Flinn - Neighborhood Church of Redding, Redding, CA

goforthconsulting.co

9. Carol Miller - Redding Seventh Day Adventist Church, Redding, CA

reddingadventist.org

10. Robin Laney - Citylight Church, Omaha, NE

citylightomaha.org

11. Jerry Mapes - Redding Christian Fellowship, Redding, CA

rcfellowship.org

12.   Carleen Dugan - Attends Vintage Grace Church, El Dorado Hills, CA

Leads groups through the Rice Foundation.

ricefoundation.us

The following participants are either current missionaries or retired:

1.   Emma Hawthorne - Serves with Hard Places Community in Cambodia

2. Marcia Braun - Retired missionary

3. Jenee Siems - Formerly served with YWAM and Hard Places Community in Cambodia

4. Marie Foote - Currently serving with World Venture in Costa Rica

5. Julie Bock - Currently serving with Assemblies of God in Spain

6. Tanya Aderman - Currently serving with Assemblies of God in Cambodia

7. Rich and Elisa Brown - Currently serving with Inca Link in Peru, Ecuador and Colombia

8.   Otto and April Habeger - Currently serving with Wycliffe Bible Translators in South Sudan.

Below is a travel testimony from one of my survey participants. Stephen Newman is a pastor at First Baptist Church in Lodi, CA. I asked him to share his experience with missions and the pros and cons of being older when going on trips.

My name is Pastor Stephen Newman, and I made my first overseas mission trip in 1981, traveling with a mission executive to Taiwan, India, Sri Lanka, Singapore, Indonesia and the

Philippines. Everywhere I went I saw huge spiritual needs. I also saw the inequality of distribution of resources. I was one of five pastors in a church in Idaho. On my trip I met pastors who had 5 churches by themselves. I also learned that the brain drain is a big problem for churches in the developing world. When their pastors go to western countries for Bible college or seminary, most never return. If they do, many now need to be supported at western levels and send their children to western schools for education. Having tasted the comforts, securities and opportunities of more developed countries, they do not want to go back.

A missionary serving in Singapore with this executive's organization recommended me to Singapore Bible College as a faculty member. This led to serving in Singapore for six years before the needs of my family brought me back stateside. With five children, I had to focus the next ten years to ministry to my church and my family. As the children began to grow up and move out of the house, the opportunities for travel increased. In 1999 my wife and I traveled to Siberia where I taught in a non-accredited Bible College. In 2003, I traveled to the Czech Republic to teach a two week course on apologetics for Campus Crusade for Christ. My wife went that same summer to Albania to show the "Jesus" film in rural villages. I loved the Czech Republic and offered myself to God to continue in these short term trips to Eastern Europe. My Crusade contact had told me that these opportunities should continue. In 2005 my wife and I traveled to Cameroon to speak at a missionary retreat for our denominational missionaries in that country and to help them with some team building issues.

In 2006 I saw a blurb in our denominational missions newsletter about needing teachers for pastoral training program in the Philippines, where the denomination had put together a program for local pastors without any formal theological training. I felt God's tug because I was familiar with ministry in South East Asia and had years of experience in theological education so I volunteered to go teach. It was not Eastern Europe. It was the tropics – hot and humid all day and all night.

But this is where the need was. The programming in Eastern Europe with Crusade changed and I was not asked to return. I had to remind myself that I was not going to be comfortable, but to meet needs. I have now taught at the center in the Philippines five times while serving as a senior pastor in America.

In 2009, my wife and I traveled to India where our church has some ministry going on. I learned that several of the short-termers who went to our site really had nothing to contribute and some were even a drain on the local missionary. My wife and I taught in conferences in three cities. A concern for children from poor families who end up in domestic servitude before they are ten because their families cannot afford to send them to school began a scholarship program for some of these children. As it grew, it go too big and cumbersome to monitor scholarships for dozens of kids in various places so the ministry evolved into a school. We raised money through a big Christmas project to erect school buildings and now give free education at this school rather than give out scholarship money. Education is "free" in India, but kids need to buy their own school uniforms, books, and sometimes even desks, all of which makes education impossible for poor families. We now have 130 students at our school and the whole operation is funded by our church. The school is overseen by a capable group of volunteers from our church, including our elder board chairman. To pay for school board visits to the school every 18 months, the school board runs a specialty coffee bar at church and the proceeds are used to fund their travel.

In 2011 I returned to Singapore to teach a one week Doctor of Ministry course. Many students were from beyond Singapore, but they all returned to their own countries and would not have the opportunity to immigrate to Singapore. With my many contacts from before, my wife and I conducted marriage seminars on the weekends before and after and I preached in churches pastored by former students.

In 2013 I spent a week near Guadalajara, Mexico with a missionary our church supports who has a youth center. Three of us went on the trip. I taught the staff, spoke at an outreach event and participated in activities with the youth.

Around this time our church became connected to a missionary in Tanzania and has sent numerous short-term missionaries to serve there. One group did contract work, but their structure fell down about seven years later. Others served in the primary school run by the mission. eight of us have gone to teach two week classes in their Bible College. After the first two pastors returned from teaching in the Bible College and explained their perception of the great needs there, I felt inspired by the Holy Spirit and said we should send two pastors a year there to teach and fund this through collecting bottles and cans for recycling. We have been able to do this so far for six years. I have taught in the Bible College in 2012 and 2015. My wife and I taught a marriage seminar one year and she did medical work during the second visit.

What are the pros and cons of serving on these short-term trips after 55? I am now 67 and am scheduled to make another trip to the youth center next year and to teach in a seminary in Ukraine in 2018. I will be putting together a team for the Mexico trip where we will paint the whole facility, do some English tutoring for their after school program and be involved in their sports programs in the afternoons. I will also do Bible teaching for the staff and for the youth.

As I get older, travel is a bit more uncomfortable and maybe my energy is slightly diminished. The key to motivation for the discomforts and sacrifices of such trips is to find a ministry for which you are equipped and can make a meaningful con-tribution. My wife was really bothered by the long flights on our last mission trip and really doesn't want to fly more than 10 hours at a time without spending the night somewhere and letting her body recover. We will see how that might work out. With extra age comes extra experience and, hopefully, extra wisdom.

Our church is exploring a new ministry we will call "Vacations with a Purpose." These will be self-funded trips that will give some mission exposure. For such trips we don't have to do a cost/benefit analysis because we will be asking people to fund themselves rather than have them raise funds to basically go and have a look-see without much of a direct contribution.

Notes

1. Steve Corbett and Brian Fikkert, *Helping without Hurting in Short-term missions*, (Chicago, IL: Moody Publishers 2014)

2. Matthew Backholer, *How to Plan, Prepare and Successfully Complete*, (United Kingdom: ByFaith Media in association with MissionsNow.co.uk 2016)

3. David Platt, *Radical Together*, (Colorado Springs, CO: Multnomah Books 2011)

4. David A Livermore, *Serving with Eyes Wide Open*, (Grand Rapids, MI: Baker Books 2013)

5. Chris Eaton and Kim Hurst, *Team Member's Manual Vacations with a purpose*, (Canada 2003)

About the Author

I'm Vicky Albaugh, I'm a child of God. God has blessed me and I'm a wife, mother and grand-mother. My greatest role in life has been being a mother. My awesome husband of 35 years is Dean. My sons are Ryan, Travis and Austin and my grandkids are Caleb and Paisley. I have 2 great daughter-in-laws also. Ryan is married to Megan and they are parents to Caleb and Paisley. Travis is married to Emily.

I've been a Christian since I was 13 and have always loved missions. I have gone on a few mission trips, but I would like to go on many more in my life. Since I'm over 55, I feel the urgency to go and make a difference for the Kingdom of God. I would also like to invite you to fulfill your dream of going on at least 1 short-term mission trip. I have written this book to encourage all of us to be open and willing to be used by the Lord. I also have a blog where I share information about missions, travel tips and stories from those of us that have been on mission trips.

Please join me at travelwithpurpose55.com.

Thank you so much for downloading or buying my book about short-term mission trips. I'd really appreciate it if you enjoyed the book that you go back to Amazon to leave a good review.

Remember to get out there from the couch to the mission field!

You can share your stories at www.travelwithpurpose55.com and you can always contact me with any questions at travel55plus@gmail.com

God bless you!

Vicky